THE JAR &

THE JAR & THE JUG

Retelling Bible stories
Old Testament

Joanna Love

wild goose
publications

www.**ionabooks**.com

First published 2024 by
Wild Goose Publications
Suite 9, Fairfield
1048 Govan Road, Glasgow G51 4XS, Scotland
A division of Iona Community Trading CIC
Limited Company Reg. No. SC156678
www.ionabooks.com

ISBN 978-1-80432-329-8

Cover photo © Joanna Love

The publishers gratefully acknowledge the support of the Drummond Trust,
3 Pitt Terrace, Stirling FK8 2EY in producing this book.

Overseas distribution
Australia: Willow Connection Pty Ltd, 1/13 Kell Mather Drive,
Lennox Head NSW 2478
New Zealand: Pleroma, Higginson Street, Otane 4170, Central Hawkes Bay

Printed in the UK by Page Bros (Norwich) Ltd

MIX
Paper | Supporting
responsible forestry
FSC
www.fsc.org   FSC® C023114

Contents

Introduction

'Story is the lifeblood of faith. In story we can tell the truth and speak with honesty about things for which there are not yet words. Story contains mystery and is the poetry that forms faith. Stories grow as we grow and can reveal new truths at different times in our lives. Giving stories to people is one of the most important things we can do in sharing our faith. Children and adults hold stories in their being and keep coming back to them throughout life. Our culture is stored in story. The same is true for our faith.'

You'll find these words repeated by way of introduction in each issue of *Spill the Beans*, the Scottish-flavoured worship and learning resources born in 2009, brainchild of my creative friend Rev. Roddy Hamilton. I still remember the evening Roddy approached me at the end of a worship event in Glasgow that year. 'Jo, I've got this idea about getting a group of folk together to do some writing to resource worship …'

Everything in this book began as a contribution to Spill the Beans. What a joy it has been to be part of this team, doing my bit as one of three 'retellers' – tussling with tales from the Bible and playing with ways to retell them that let us look from a different angle, bring our imaginations to what is going on, and deepen our curiosity so that we stay a while with the people and events described. Because these are our stories, and if we can get inside them, they can get inside us!

Whenever I've had the chance to ask people about reading the Bible, I've heard many admit how awkward, inaccessible and off-putting it can feel as we try to get into its pages. How often have the Spill team tussled with scripture passages ourselves and reacted with speechless stares around the room followed by, 'Well, what do we do with this?!'

In these pages, then, are some of the things I have done after a good team tussling! They are offered as ways in to the intriguing or impenetrable, heart-warming or horrendous, alien or alluring happenings we meet in the Bible. They have been road-tested in congregations and I hope adapted and reshaped by others.

Thanks to Roddy and all the Spill the Beans team for the invitation and ongoing motivation to delve into, tear apart and piece together all kinds of stories, by which we live.

Joanna Love

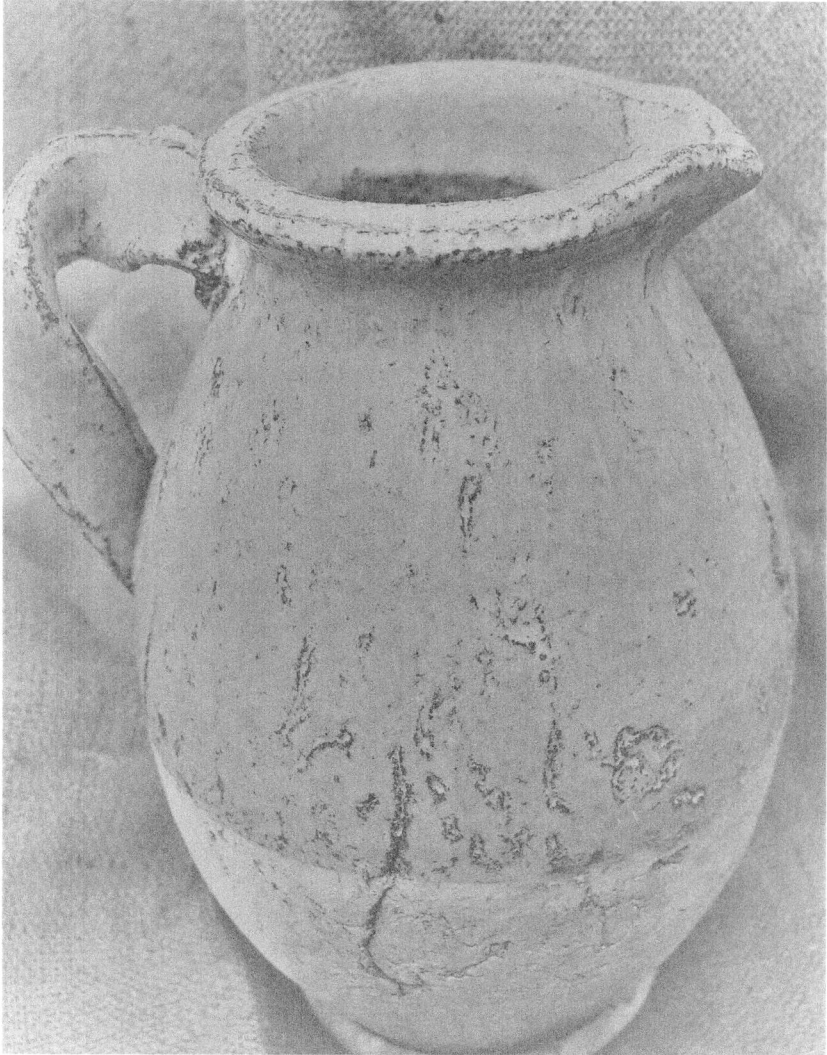

GENESIS

Genesis 2:15–17; 3:1–7

WHY THE SNAKE WAS SAD

Well, what would *you* have asked God for, as the one thing that makes you an animal who is different from any other? Would you have wanted purple feathers, or the longest tail, or to be the cuddliest pet for children? By the time I got my turn to ask, all the good things were gone. There were no wings left. No fins or fur or paws or claws. There weren't even any *legs* left. So I wasn't going to fly or walk or run. What made me special? My very long belly and being able to open my mouth so wide I could eat an egg whole. Which is not very exciting …

Then God said there were still some 'personal strengths' on offer. You know the kind of thing … great sense of humour, courage, good listener, very caring … but who would take notice of a long-bellied, egg-swallowing creature who is 'very caring' or 'will really make you laugh'?

'What else is left?' I asked God.

'Animal with the loudest burp, the deadliest sting, the smelliest smell … the most cowardly creature, the most cranky, the most crafty and cunning …'

Aha! *Crafty and cunning!* Clever and sly! Slyly wily! But I thought the fox had got this one. Could I really be more cunning than a fox?!

So I thought I'd have to try out this new gift. How could I prove I really was cunning?

Of all the other creatures in the garden, my favourites were the man creature and the woman creature. They were in charge of the garden and they looked after it well. Every day they made sure we all had good food and were getting on well. I liked it best in the evenings just before God took a stroll to chat with them, because sometimes the woman creature would bother to stop and chat with me. She didn't mind that there's nothing much to me but one long belly. She would tell me about all the things I couldn't see in the garden – the tall flowers, the fruits on the trees, and how it felt to climb up into the high branches to watch the sunset with the man creature.

We talked about God too, and what a wonderful garden God had made for us. We talked about God's Special Tree, the beautiful tree that no one was to touch. The woman creature always tiptoed and hushed herself when she passed it by, and she always smiled a big smile when God said, 'Thank you for remembering not to touch that tree!'

So that was what gave me the idea about being cunning. It would be the hardest challenge of all!

The following evening, there she was as usual, the lovely woman creature coming across the garden to see me. 'Hello, snake! I must tell you about the new fruits that are growing in the garden! I know you can't see them from down there in the grass. Well, they're big and round and pinky red and very shiny. They're so beautiful!'

So I tried very hard to be very sly. 'And … ermm … did God *really* tell you not to eat the fruit from the trees in the garden?' I held my breath, feeling very foolish. What a silly question. I didn't sound sly and crafty at all!

The woman creature looked at me, puzzled. 'Of course we can eat the fruit!' she laughed. 'Just not the fruit from God's Special Tree. It's not to be touched, as you know very well, dear snake!'

I decided to try one more time, and with all the cunning I could muster, I said in my slyest voice, 'God only told you not to touch it because if you eat it you'll know everything that God knows!'

As soon as I'd said it I wished the ground would swallow me as easily as I could swallow an egg. She's going to laugh at me, I thought, she might even stop being my friend, oh what a daft thing to say. It's no fun being cunning after all …

'Everything that *God* knows…? *Everything* that God knows…?' The woman creature sounded like she was dreaming, as though a thousand thoughts were tumbling through her mind all at once. Then all of a sudden she got up and ran off. I tried to follow as fast as I could, slithering and twisting in the grass but quickly getting left behind. By the time I caught up, the woman creature and the man creature were standing beside God's Special Tree, holding pieces of its fruit in their hands, and the fruit had been bitten, and they were *munching* on the fruit God had told them *not to touch*!

Di-sas-ter!

I covered my eyes with my long belly and couldn't bear to look. Any minute now God would turn up. I buried my head in the grass and groaned; oh God, I should have taken the great sense of humour after all …

There were voices and footsteps and I dared to have a peek. It was still just the man creature and the woman creature standing there, but they had … they had … what on earth *did* they have? There were *leaves* all over them! I thought for a moment God had answered my prayer and given me that sense of humour, because I laughed out loud.

When God found out, it wasn't so funny. God was sad. The woman creature and the man creature were sad. I was sad. And somehow everything changed.

I only meet the woman creature outside the garden now. We're still friends. We talk about the choices we make, and how you have to think about what will happen if you choose to do this, and what will happen if you choose to do that. It's a bit like going on a journey. We should know.

Genesis 3

ANOTHER DAY OF CREATION

There was evening
and there was morning,
another day in the garden …

beautiful trees
beautiful food
beautiful creatures
it was very good

and there was tricking
and there was manipulation
and there was tempting
and there was evaluation

perception pleasing
taste buds fired
death threat diminished
wisdom desired

and there was considering
and there was choice
and there was believing
the deceiving voice

fruit taken
eyes unshuttered
nakedness felt
bodies covered

and there was hiding
and there was shame
and there was cursing
and there was blame

head and heel enemies
childbirth pain
thorns and thistles
sweat and strain

and there was mortality
and there was ejection
and there was retrospective
angelic protection

And there was evening
and there was morning,
the first day out in the world ...

THE CHERRY TREE (YOUNGER RETELLING)

One sunny day in the garden of a big house in a little village, two squirrel friends, Smudge and Skippy, were scampering among the trees looking for some lunch. There were so many choices of what to eat – the juiciest apples from the apple tree, some leftover cat food in the dish at the back door, or maybe some bird seed that had spilled onto the grass under the bird feeder.

Smudge decided it was a nice day for a fruity lunch. And he wanted to taste a crunchy, munchy apple before their squirrel friends Dasher and Dodge came along. Hop, scamper, hop went Smudge. Over towards the apple tree, weaving around the other trees on the way. Past the pear tree, past the plum tree, round the … THUD!

Oh! What is this?! Smudge had run right into a fence that had never been there before! It was a very hard fence. A very solid fence. A very smooth and shiny fence. A very high fence, made of metal!

Suddenly Skippy appeared beside her friend. 'Are you OK?'

'Yes,' said Smudge, a bit dazed. 'What's this fence here for?'

Smudge slowly got up and walked along the fence. Round and round in a circle it went. All the way around the cherry tree. How strange! A new fence that was solid and hard and smooth and shiny and high and metal. It was the kind of fence that no squirrel could climb! And it went all the way round the cherry tree.

Smudge and Skippy loved cherries, but they had never, ever tasted a cherry from the tree in this lovely big garden. Oh no! The cherry tree was the gardener's favourite tree; all the squirrels in the village knew that. Smudge and Skippy and their friends Dodge and Dasher knew it. Even the birds knew not to peck any cherries. And Skippy and Smudge certainly didn't want to be chased away from the garden for eating fruit from the gardener's favourite tree. There were plenty of other nice things to eat, so it had never been any bother to stay away from the cherry tree, even when the cherries were at their ripest and reddest and juiciest!

'What's this fence here for?' asked Smudge again, swishing his bushy tail in puzzlement.

'Haven't you heard?' said Skippy. 'Dodge took three cherries yesterday!'

'He did what?!'

'Yep! He climbed right up there, took three ripe, red, juicy cherries, and ate them!'

'But it's the gardener's favourite tree! We've always agreed we would leave it alone!'

'I know, and Dodge knew it too. But he did it. He ate the cherries. So the gardener came and built this fence to make sure that no squirrel will ever have the chance of taking any cherries again!'

Smudge was upset. 'Oh, why did Dodge do that? This horrible fence spoils the garden! And my head hurts from crashing into it. We can't even properly see the cherry tree with its beautiful fruit any more … It's not fair! Dodge does the one thing we've always agreed not to do, and the garden is spoiled for everyone.'

Skippy gently stroked Smudge's sore head with her paw.

'I know. I think the fence is ugly and horrible too. Dasher said that the gardener caught Dodge in the cherry tree and chased him away. It's the first time any squirrel has ever been chased away from this lovely garden.'

'What can we do, Skippy?' cried Smudge. 'I want Dodge to come back and play here. I want the gardener to be sure that none of us will climb up the cherry tree again. And I want this fence to be taken away. What can we do?'

Ask the children what they think Smudge and Skippy could do, and if they think it would make the situation better. Have they ever seen a friend behave like Dodge did? What happened?

Genesis 6:16–22

AFTER THE FLOOD

A monologue by Shem, son of Noah, in a mood of anger and sarcasm at first, more thoughtful towards end.

It'll be different next time. If there is a next time. Dad is of course saying there will be no next time. Apparently that's a promise. Never again. If I'm in charge, it will definitely not be a repeat performance. I won't just stand there without arguing back. I'll have something to say about it! There's going to be a flood, but our little tribe will be fine, so that's no problem then? It's just tough luck for all the rest? I don't think so! Honour your father? How can I honour a man who didn't even put up a fight for the sake of our own neighbours, let alone those in the poor drowned cities we'll never have a chance to know? What about my poor old friend Aphas? More of a brother than Ham and Japheth have ever been. What about that lamb he loved like a child, and all Aphas' family and their flocks?

So, the waters are subsiding and we have survived. We're all right, so everything's all right? Thank God the disaster happened to someone else? Thank God our lives were worth saving? Nobody else's lives really mattered, right?

We can't yet see what flooding does to the world, but we're beginning to smell it. Does Dad naively think the sea will just go back to where it belongs and leave everything green and shiny and fresh? Does he really see those strange bands of colour in the sky as proof of a happy ever after? They look to me like an upturned arc … *an upturned ark.* God, what a warning! Why should the few stay afloat while the many go under? Who are we to just batten down the hatches while the land is laid to waste? Who has the right to build a cocoon and hide while others have nowhere to run? Lord, you've placed your upturned ark in the sky … and you've warned us, it will be different next time.

Genesis 12:1–9

STOPPING

A dialogue between Lot and Abram, to follow the Bible reading.

Lot: Where next?

Abram: Nowhere, just yet …

Lot: Let me guess. You're stopping again?

Abram: That's right. I'm stopping again.

Lot: Don't you want to see the land?

Abram: That's why I'm stopping. To see the land.

Lot: Not this land. I mean the land God's promised us.

Abram: Well, this could be it. Or some of it.

Lot: You said that at the last place we stopped.

Abram: That's right.

Lot: So why didn't we stay there?

Abram: Stopping and staying isn't everything.

Lot: *(sigh)* You like being on the move then?

Abram: I like being on the move, yes …

Lot: Come on then, let's get on to where we're going!

Abram: There's a time for getting going, and a time for stopping.

Lot: How long are we stopping for this time then?

Abram: I don't know.

Lot: Let me guess – long enough to build another altar?

Abram: What a great idea. Yes, we should build another altar.

Lot: Uncle Abram, why do you build all these altars?

Abram: It helps me to pray.

Lot: But you never say anything. You just pick up stones.

Abram: That's right. The searching and the picking up and the building is my prayer. Words aren't everything.

Lot: But then you just sit there doing nothing.

Abram: That's when I do some thinking.

Lot: Thinking it's another great altar you've just built?

Abram: Thinking about God, mostly.

Lot: So what makes you get up and get going again?

Abram: I don't know. But thinking's not everything. There's a time for travelling again, moving on.

Lot: So, where next?

Abram: I don't know…

Lot: Doesn't God let you know, after all that prayer and thinking?

Abram: Knowing's not everything.

Lot: But don't you ever ask questions, Uncle Abram?

Abram: Oh yes. Just as well answers aren't everything!

Lot: But God made you a promise.
        Don't you want to know how it's going to be fulfilled –
        how you're going to be a blessing?

Abram: Yes, but even promises aren't everything.

Lot: So what's the most important thing then?

Abram: It's all important.
            The stopping and the travelling,
            the searching and the building,
            the praying and the thinking,
            the words and the altars,
            the sitting and the silence,
            the doing nothing and the moving on,
            the knowing and the not knowing,
            the questions and the answers,
            the land and the promise and the being a blessing …
            it's all important.

Lot: *(after a pause)* Should I give you some peace and quiet now,
            Uncle?

Abram: Only if you want to, my son.
            Peace and quiet isn't everything!

Genesis 12:1–4a

PENSIONER ON PILGRIMAGE

Monologue from Abraham, recapping journey on reaching the oak at Moreh.

So this is the place I've waited all these years to see. This is the place Dad went on and on about, even though he really knew nothing about it.

Canaan. Canaan.

This was my Dad's dream, long before it was mine. Oh yes, getting here from Haran wasn't the start of our journey! It was Dad who upped and left home, persuading me and Sarai and my young nephew Lot to come with him.

I've often wondered what voice he heard, what vision he had. Was he prompted by God at all? Was he reacting out of grief? My youngest brother died at our family home in Ur. Next we know, Dad is for leaving the place forever.

We followed the river upstream to the northwest. I never would have believed the Euphrates flowed from so far inland! Worlds we had never seen or imagined opened up to us over those months on the move. There were times we stopped of course, and set up camp for a while. Sarai always amazed us with what she could cook up from the vegetation around us and some meat from the little flock we herded with us.

There were days we loved that nomadic existence. It makes you travel light, and trust the earth. It was then that we faced such disappointment too ... never knowing the blessing of a child on the way. Was God saying we had got it all wrong with leaving home? But you couldn't say that, if you knew my father. His journey upriver was like a journey up out of sorrow, walking by faith. He taught me so much ...

But we longed to stop and settle too; to call somewhere 'home' again. And Dad got tired. 'I'll take you halfway, son,' he used to say. 'I'll make it halfway, and then you must keep on and see what God has promised.'

Arriving at Haran was amazing. We hadn't seen so many people in months! Sarai made friends with all the women straight away. Lot had grown up so much since leaving Ur, he was a great help in building our new house, making new pots, planting vegetables and keeping our goats and sheep well.

We never thought we'd stay so long in Haran. The years rolled on and we were a tight unit, with Lot never marrying, and still no children for me and Sarai, and Dad ageing, but never letting me forget this was only halfway, that the time would come to move on again. We both knew it wouldn't happen while he was still with us. And after he died, sure enough I got restless, and I yearned for the mountains, for the earth and the air, to be walking day after day, just as we had when Dad was fit and fired up with the Spirit of God ... and maybe I did feel it then, the voice and the vision inside that you can't ignore ...

Others came with us this time, a wee band of friends we'd made, some true companions and some just plain curious about the divine promise we claimed to trust. It was so different not having Dad to lead the way. I had to figure out for myself where God was leading us, to the south, a little east, and nearer the sea. I don't know how I knew that this was it ... Canaan ... but we kept going until this huge oak tree was in our path. You must know how sacred the oak tree is to us, so it seems like a sign.

Well, here I am. My father's dream? I hope I've got it right. Yes, I hope I've done you proud, Dad. And I pray to God to keep showing me the way.

Genesis 18:1–15

GIVING BIRTH TO LAUGHTER

A monologue by Sarah, to follow the reading.

So I laughed. Yes, I laughed when I heard. Laughing was my default reaction after all those years. It's what everyone told me to do. Look for the things that make you laugh. Find the things that bring a moment's lightness, a brief respite. God knows I needed those moments. And yes, I found them. I learned to forget, to step outside the guilt and the pain, to be lost in the fleeting respite, caught up in the wonder of the spring rain, the flowers in the desert, the look in my husband's eyes, those rare times he still gazed at me with love and not pity.

For long years, laughter never failed me. I could even turn it on as I watched all the mothering around me, other women's children taking their first steps, running into my arms while they were still too young to understand my shame.

Did I trust God's laughable promise? Did Abraham trust, even as he fell into sardonic mirth when he heard the first time? Of course we sat down and looked at it seriously. If it's God's promise, I reasoned, I'll cope, even with Hagar's belly swelling. It all made sense. And then I laughed. I laughed at myself when no one could hear me. Who was I kidding? How would I cope? How did it make sense? What was God doing? What had I done wrong?

It all happened so easily for her. Abraham loved the boy – his boy – and I saw the joy in him that I had never been able to bring. It was too much. I called on the laughter but it would not come. I searched for it in the winking stars, in the smell of good soup, in the faces of friends, but it would not come.

It came with the visitors' news. The cakes were baking and I was dusting the flour from my hands when I heard them speak my name. How did they know my name, and why care to speak of me? 'Sarah shall have a son.' They heard me laughing, and would not let me deny it! Praise God, nor was there any denying the pleasure, or the promise, or my pregnant old body, or the tears of joy in my husband's eyes when we held our son. What did we name him? We named him Laughter.

Laughing and crying (younger retelling)

Have you ever laughed when you wanted to cry? Or cried so much that you couldn't cry any more? Poor old Sarah cried for years. She lived a long, long time ago, and she cried because she had never had a baby. It made her so sad. In those days, women thought that the nicest thing that could ever happen was to have a baby. Poor Sarah spent years watching all her friends with their little girls and boys, growing up and growing older, and she never became a mum herself. Eventually she stopped crying and often found herself laughing even when she was sad. All her friends said, 'Sarah! Cheer up! There are still lots of happy things to do, lots of beautiful things to look at, lots of friendly people who love you!' And they were right. Sarah used to watch the birds flying and the flowers blossoming and for a while she was happy. But the sadness was always there. How she wished she had a family.

When Sarah and her husband were very old, they had some visitors one day. Sarah was busy baking bread when she heard one of the visitors say that by the time they visited again next year, Sarah would be a mum! She would have a baby boy! 'Hahaha!' chuckled Sarah. 'As if I'm going to believe that now!' But the visitors weren't joking. It was a special message from God and it was true! By the time they came back again to see Sarah, she was holding her own little son Isaac in her arms! Sarah and her husband were over the moon with joy. And can you guess what the name 'Isaac' means? *(Let the children try guessing!)* It means 'Laughter'!

Genesis 32:22–30

Wrestling in the night

He is alone. He has chosen to be alone. Darkness falls early and the sky is clear. The air is cool and still. He sits on a rock by the stream, listening to the steady music of its gurgling water, to his own heartbeat, to the welcome emptiness of the night. He reaches for a handful of stones and tosses them one by one, hearing the gentle plop as the surface breaks and swallows them. He breathes deeply, his ribcage rising and then falling with a long audible sigh.

A sudden moving shape has him on his feet, poised, muscles quivering. No words, no weapons, but a naked brute force rams into him with ferocious energy. Thick arms claim his torso and a deft foot seeks to buckle him behind the knee. With a strength fuelled by anger and alarm, he is not overcome. They are locked in an unyielding grip, heaving and sweating, neither giving way. This is not the assailant he expected. This flesh is smooth, not the ruddy, hairy brother betrayed. This breath smells neither of spice nor wine. These muscles are well-defined yet unblemished. This fight is eerily equal and exhaustingly long. Who is this? He cannot yet see the other's face and the wrestling and writhing goes on and on. The sky shows signs of dawn and still he is not beaten, he will not submit. Neither does the other relent or release. They are locked again in frozen fury when one blow hammers his hip, as hard as a falling boulder, wrenching the joint as he yells out.

The other speaks at last. 'Let me go.'

'I will not let you go,' he counters adamantly, 'unless you bless me.'

The other speaks again, a loaded question that hangs in the air between their aching chests.

'What is your name?'

Will he give the stranger his very self? Is this the way to learning who has come to him, struggled with him, wounded him? 'Jacob,' he hears himself say, and no sooner is it spoken than it is taken from him. 'You will be Israel – for you have prevailed against God and people.'

But it is still as Jacob that he demands to know, 'And what is your name?' There is no answer, but there before him is the full sight of the other's face, and there he is blessed. Peniel is the new name he gives the place where it happens. 'For I have seen God,' he whispers to the rising sun, 'and I am still alive.'

A GOOD FIGHT? (YOUNGER RETELLING)

After the story, encourage the children to share their reactions: What do they think about the story? What do they wonder about? Imagine being Jacob. Why do you think God came and had this 'good fight' with him?

Getting into a fight is a bad idea. Someone will get hurt. Maybe both of you will get hurt. And it usually leaves you feeling angry and upset, and maybe humiliated. There's always a winner and a loser, but even if you win, it can still make you feel bad. Could there ever be a fight with no winner and no loser? Could there ever be a fight that didn't leave anyone feeling bad, but actually made something good happen?

In the Bible there's a strange story about a strange fight. It all started with Jacob, who was spending the night alone by a stream, waiting to meet his long-lost brother. Jacob and his brother had fallen out with each other years before, and Jacob was sure his brother still hated him.

In the middle of the night, someone arrived and started fighting with Jacob. It was like wrestling – the man just grabbed hold of Jacob and they pushed each other around, each of them trying to be stronger than the other. But the stranger could not beat Jacob. And Jacob could not beat the stranger. They shoved and heaved and pushed and struggled for hours and hours. Nobody was winning. Nobody was losing. Jacob wouldn't let go of the man. The man wouldn't let go of Jacob. Jacob grew exhausted but he wouldn't give in! The stranger grew exhausted but he wouldn't give in! On and on they wrestled and fought. Jacob began to realise this was not like any other fight. It didn't feel as if the stranger hated him. It didn't feel as if the stranger was going to make a fool of him, or that he was really trying to get the better of him.

But suddenly the stranger hit out at Jacob. He thumped Jacob on the hip. Ouch! Jacob had a limp for the rest of his life. But the limp meant he could never forget that night. He never wanted to forget it. Because when the fight ended, the stranger blessed Jacob and gave him a new name. 'You will be called "Israel",' said the stranger, 'a name that means you struggled with God and with people and you didn't give in.'

So was it God who had been there wrestling with Jacob? Can God come and fight with someone and make something good come out of it? What a strange experience. But for once it didn't leave anyone feeling bad after a fight. Jacob had a limp, but he had a blessing. He had seen God face to face!

Genesis 38:6–26

TAMAR

Tamar. A woman in a patriarchal world. In such a world, it was a good thing to get married.

Plan A – Tamar married Er. They would have children and live happily ever after.

But Er let her down. He was not a good man, and he died before becoming a dad.

Plan B – Er's nearest brother, Onan, would marry Tamar and they would have children and live happily ever after.

But Onan let her down. He knowingly cheated Tamar out of her chances of parenthood.

Plan C – Er's youngest brother, Shelah, would marry Tamar and they would have children and live happily ever after.

But Shelah was young and Tamar had to wait, widowed and childless, in her own father's house. Tamar waited. Shelah grew up. Plan C – ready now?

But Tamar's father-in-law, Judah, let her down. Judah did not give Tamar in marriage to his youngest son Shelah.

Plan D – A risky plan; a proactive plan; a desperate plan; a survival plan but a plan that could cost her her life if it failed. A last resort by a woman in a patriarchal world, let down by one man after another after another. Tamar dressed up as a prostitute and her father-in-law used her, not knowing or caring who she was. This was how far she had to go to make her case, to become a mother, to have a future, to show up the failure of those who should have looked after her.

Courageous Tamar; foremother of Christ.

Genesis 43:1–5; 45:1–18

THE CUPBEARER MUSES

Well well, young Hebrew, look at you now. Not so young but still as sure of your dreams. First time we met we were in the cells together, condemned men, not knowing if we would rot there, forgotten and unforgiven. I knew you'd been a slave but you were always quick to say how you'd ruled your master's household. I must admit it wasn't hard to believe you, seeing how you impressed the prison guard and gained a position of oversight even in jail! Chief among prisoners. Huh! Not much of an honour, but you took what you could get.

And I knew you were a foreigner. Though if you don't mind me saying, if I'd had a kid brother with dreams of grandeur like yours, I might have happily sold him to the highest bidder too.

You asked me, on my release, to put in a good word for you – a fair request, but I never did. Not until that morning after Pharaoh's nightmares. Little did I know what was going to come of it for you. Pulled out of the cells one minute, and paraded through the city in all the king's regalia the next. I remember standing by as the chariot rumbled past the palace, wondering how anyone could cope with such a sudden change of fortunes. It was hard enough for me, coming back from the dungeon to be reinstated; trying to get back to normal when I'd thought I might be executed. But you – from powerless to unspeakably powerful in a flash; invisible captive to instant celebrity. But you've handled it, dreamer boy, stepping into the leadership and the limelight, back at the top all over again. All those dreams of greatness coming true, it seems.

Slave boy, jailbird, national hero, dreamer ... then out of the blue, you alarm the whole palace with a breakdown into unholy wailing! Oh, the rumours that flew. Joseph's lost it. He's ill. He's dying. He's possessed. He's exhausted.

Now we've all heard the great twist in your story. Your brothers came. But they did not know you. You broke down when you told them. And now your father is on his way. Is this your family reconciled, my friend? Did you ever dream of that?

BROTHERS AND SISTERS (YOUNGER RETELLING)

Have a time of discussion with the children about their brothers and sisters. Invite them to share stories about some of the best fun they have had with their siblings, how they have helped or been helped by them in special ways, and any times of arguing and falling out. Tell some stories of your own, if you have any brothers or sisters. Explore the reality of jealousy between siblings, and how any of us might wish we weren't the youngest or oldest or in the middle.

Do you remember the story in the Bible about the family with lots of sisters and brothers? One of the youngest, Joseph, was his Dad's favourite, which made his brothers very jealous. He had lots of dreams about how he would grow up to be more important than his brothers! Do you remember what his brothers did to him? They sold Joseph as a slave and he was carried away to another country – Egypt. But what happened to him there? He was a slave for a few years and then he ended up in prison. But he was released from prison because he helped the King of Egypt to understand some bad dreams. The king's dreams were a warning that all the food in the country was going to run out because there would be no harvests for seven years. What a warning! Joseph was given the job of organising food storage while the harvests were still good. That way, no one would go hungry during the famine.

But far away in Joseph's old homeland, his family didn't know about the food warning, and they became very hungry. Eventually they went to Egypt to beg for food, but they had no idea it would be Joseph who was there to help them! They probably thought he was already dead. So they didn't even recognise him when they saw him.

Oh my. The last time these brothers had all been together, there was all that jealousy and bad feeling. What do you think happened when Joseph told his brothers who he was?

Invite the children to share their thoughts and ideas about what Joseph did, how his brothers might have reacted, and how the family made friends again. What would have made this an easy or difficult thing to do?

EXODUS

Exodus 16:1–8

WHO'S TO BLAME?

A grumbling Israelite challenges Moses on the food crisis. Moses stays upbeat, with occasional appropriate sarcasm!

Israelite: I'm hungry.

Moses: Yep.

Israelite: We're all hungry.

Moses: I can see that.

Israelite: You'll have to do something.

Moses: Me? Why me?

Israelite: Because this is all your fault, that's why.

Moses: No it isn't.

Israelite: Yes it is. You brought us out here!

Moses: No I didn't!

Israelite: Yes you did. You and your grand, stupid idea.

Moses: It wasn't my idea.

Israelite: So why did you do it?

Moses: I didn't do it. God did it.

Israelite: But you told us everything would be all right.

Moses: No I didn't. I had no idea what would happen.

Israelite: But you've wandered about in places like this before.

Moses: Yep, I've been in the desert more than the rest of you.

Israelite: You knew there would be no food here.

Moses: Yep, I knew there's not much to eat in a desert ...

Israelite: So it's your fault we're all hungry!

Moses: I'm hungry too. What do you want me to do?

Israelite: You could take us back to Egypt.

Moses: Great idea.

Israelite: Find us some food then.

Moses: That's not my job.

Israelite: Well, whose job is it?

Moses: It's God's job. Go complain to God.

Israelite: What's God going to do about it?

Moses: God's going to feed you.

Israelite: What makes you say that?

Moses: God told me.

Israelite: God told you he's going to feed us?

Moses: Yes.

Israelite: When?

Moses: Tonight.

Israelite: What about tomorrow?

Moses: Yep, he'll feed you tomorrow too.

Israelite: What about the next day?

Moses: Yep. And the day after that.

Israelite: Is that a promise?

Moses: Food is on its way. Promise.

Israelite: From where?

Moses: From heaven.

Israelite: From heaven?! How can you get food from heaven?

Moses: Same way as you get rain from heaven, or so God tells me.

Israelite: How are you going to do that?

Moses: I keep telling you, I'm not going to do anything. God's going to do something.

Israelite: How can you believe that?

Moses: How can you believe we got out of Egypt?

Israelite: Well, we're here, aren't we?

Moses: And some food is about to be here too.

Israelite: What kind of food?

Moses: Some kind of bread, I think, and some kind of meat.

Israelite: No melons? No cucumbers?

Moses: You can always go back to Egypt for some of them.

Israelite: I didn't really mean the bit about Egypt.

Moses: You don't say …

Israelite: What if there's no bread or meat tonight, or tomorrow, or the next day?

Moses: *(shrugging)* Don't blame me.

ENOUGH FOR TODAY (YOUNGER RETELLING)

Once upon a long time ago, a big crowd of people was on a long journey across a desert. God loved every one of them. God had rescued them from a king who had been cruel to them. Now they were walking for miles and miles to a new country far away from the cruel king. There was one big problem about being in the desert. There was hardly anything to eat there. Oh dear. All the people became very hungry. But God loved them and cared about them. So God sent them food from heaven! God's special food was like bread, and there was enough for all the people to fill their tummy for one day. God promised to send more food the next day.

Let's imagine two friends in that big crowd – Abi and Eli. Imagine what they thought when they saw the bread after being so hungry. Abi thought … 'Did God *really* say there would be food tomorrow? What if there isn't? Maybe I should take more than enough for now, so that I'll not go hungry tomorrow.' So Abi took not just one little loaf of bread – but three! Then she met Eli. Eli had only picked up one loaf, just enough to eat for one day. Abi held out one of her extra loaves. 'Eli, take this extra food. Then we'll each have one for tomorrow!' But Eli said, 'No, Abi, don't you remember God said we should just take enough for today. If we take more than we need, someone else will still be hungry!' 'But how can we be sure there will be more tomorrow?' said Abi, hiding her extra loaf under her coat. 'I don't want to be hungry!' 'We'll be all right, Abi,' said Eli. 'God will look after us. We can trust that there will be enough food every day, just the right amount for everyone, so long as nobody starts worrying and taking more than they need!' Abi felt the extra loaf as she clutched it tightly. Maybe Eli was right. But oh dear, it was hard to believe that if everyone got just enough to eat today, God would definitely send more tomorrow. But then, what if somebody was hungry right now because of the extra bread that Abi had taken?

What do you think Abi decided to do? What would you have done if you'd been there long ago in the desert?

Exodus 17:1–7

NAME THAT PLACE

A conversation between Moses and two unnamed Israelites, to follow the reading. You could have a large signpost, somewhere in view but away from the speakers, saying 'Argue and Test'. It might be fun to also have another one ready to put up beside it at the end, saying 'High Hopes'.

A: Did you have to call it that?

Moses: What?

A: 'Argue and Test.'
        It's not a very nice name.

Moses: It wasn't very nice behaviour.

B: But we don't need reminded of that every time we go back there.

A: You've got us all squirming.
        It's ... uncomfortable ... embarrassing!

Moses: Maybe you *do* need reminded.
        Maybe I should have made you squirm a long time ago.
        Maybe that's what I did wrong.

A: What?

Moses: Yep, I wonder why it took me so long
        to *name* what you've been doing.
        You're suddenly having a proper look at yourselves.

B: Well OK, we kind of complained a bit, and weren't very trusting,
        but you didn't have to paint it up in bold letters!

Moses: Can I show you something?

A&B: What?

Moses: *(pulling out a chart)*
        Here is the map *I've* been keeping of our journey.
        I made some notes of other names along the way,

not that I painted them up in bold anywhere.
Let's go right back to day one.
Here – just past the Reed Sea ...

B: *(looking at chart)*
'Bickering'.

A: Let me see! *(looking at chart).*
Oh no, a bit further along the road you've got 'Fracas' ...

B: ... and not long after that comes 'Petty Pouting'.

A: What's this in the foothills?

B: 'Headache'.

A: And halfway along to the next wadi ...

B: Looks like 'Discord'.

A: Aw, Moses! *(Pointing at chart)*
What have you got here?

B: *(looking)* But he's right!
I remember that campsite on the plain –
'Tantrums Common' –
we deserve it!

A: What's this bit you've scored out?

Moses: Couldn't decide between 'Little Grumbles' or 'Lesser Whinings'.

A: Have we been that bad?

B: We've probably been worse!
What's this other list in the corner here?

Moses: Oh, those are the names I'm still looking forward to using.

A: Let me guess ... 'Greater Gripes'? ... or 'Full-scale Fallout'?

B: No... look! There's 'Harmony Junction'.

A: Ah ... well, we've not earned that one yet.

B: 'Reconciled'.

A: Hmm.
          Sometimes we get about halfway there.

B: 'Trusting'.

A: Long way to go!

Moses: But we'll get there. We'll get there.

B: You really think so?
          Then maybe we should name this place … 'High Hopes'.

HOT, THIRSTY, GRUMPY PEOPLE (YOUNGER RETELLING)

This is a story from long ago when Moses was leading his people away from Egypt to a new home in a better land. They had been walking through the desert for a long time and today there was no water. Not a drip drop. 'I'm thirsty!' someone said. 'Me too!' shouted another. 'Give us some water, Moses!' Soon everyone was saying it – a whole big crowd of hot, thirsty, grumpy people. 'Give us some water! Give us some water!' Moses started feeling very hot and grumpy too. What was he supposed to do to get water for all his friends in the middle of a desert? But they kept shouting, 'Give us some water! Give us some water! And tell us, is God still here with us or has God gone away and left us?!' So Moses complained to God. 'What am I supposed to do, God? What am I supposed to do for all these hot, thirsty, grumpy people? They want me to give them water but what can I do about it? And are you still with us, God? Helllloooooo? Are you still with us or have you gone away and left us?'

Well, the people were grumpy and Moses was grumpy, but God didn't get grumpy. The people thought God might have gone away and Moses thought God might have gone away, but God hadn't gone away and left them. God listened to all the hot, thirsty, grumpy people and he loved them very much; so he said to Moses, 'Follow me to that big rock over there. Hit the rock with your stick!' So Moses went to the big rock and hit it with his stick. WHOOSH! GURGLE! SPLOSSSHHH! Water came pouring out and everyone had enough to drink.

Exodus 17:1–7

WATERLESS WANDERERS

I was thirsty. Weren't we all. Have you ever been anywhere really hot and really dry, and not had any water, not a single drop? Do you know how long you can live without water? Three days, if you're lucky. And we'd been camped at Rephidim for two days when the panic started …

The first day, the men started digging for an underground spring. My mother told me and my sisters to keep out of their way. I'd asked my uncle Abidan how he knew where to dig, but this time he wasn't following any of his own clues. First, you look for natural rock pockets that hold surface water, he said. If there are none, then you look for any patches of damp sand. Then you look for any plants that are growing, even the tiniest one. Then you look for any lines of a streambed, and dig outside the sharp bends. Or last of all, if there are any cactus plants, you can cut them and suck water from the pulp inside.

My uncle's face was dark and frowning by that first sunset. There wasn't even much hope of soaking up dew in the morning, as there was nothing growing that could catch the dew.

On the second day, I told my sisters I was going to walk outside the camp and search for plants, for rock pools, anything. We spread the word to our cousins, and let the whisper grow among the children. Our mothers mostly stayed in the shade of the tents while the men organised themselves for further digging. We gathered in clusters and disappeared into the surrounding desert, keeping the camp in our sights but feeling like brave adventurers who might just save the day!

I glowed with importance as I taught the others what to look for. The smallest shoot of something green and we dived on it with bare hands, scooping down into the sand, taking turns to dig. Beneath the hot surface, the cooler layers raised our hopes, but there was no water. Again and again we thought we would feel the sand turn damp beneath our clawing fingers, but still there was no water.

'Our fathers will be praying for God to help us!' my little sister suddenly cried. 'That's what we should do too!'

Our search began again with new enthusiasm, and as one voice we recited all the prayers we knew so well. How many hours did we spend, how many places did we try, how many prayers did we chant, but still there was no water! Our tongues felt rough and our lips cracked till it was almost painful to speak. As the sun dipped towards the horizon, we threw ourselves down in an exhausted heap, scared and silent but for our heaving ribs and rasping coughs.

I pulled myself up at last and the others followed, the long line of us like defeated warriors, none of us daring to say what we desperately hoped – that we would return to find the camp rejoicing because our fathers had found what we had not. Only my little sister spoke, when she stumbled up beside me, took my hand and croaked, 'God will look after us. Remember that's what Daddy always says!'

We knew there was something very wrong as we came near the camp. More than half the tents had been taken down and our mothers were packing up our belongings. Men's voices were raised in angry argument and we could hardly take in what was happening.

'Why did he bring us here to die? Is this what the Lord wants for us, to starve and thirst in this godforsaken place?'

'He's gone ahead with the elders. They will call for us soon!'

'You fool. What can we hope for but to return to Egypt! God has abandoned us! Why rescue us from Pharaoh and kill us for want of water? A curse on Moses, a curse on him!'

A chill ran through me at my father's rage.

'Daddy! No!' It was my little sister's sobs that halted his tirade. He turned to see her running, and swept her up in his arms, his rage disintegrating into tears of his own, as he sank to the ground with his child whimpering, 'God will look after us, Daddy. God will look after us, won't he? Daddy? Won't he?'

'Gaddiel! Gaddiel!' A loud yell in the distance broke in on us. My father staggered up at the sound of his name. My uncle Abidan was running towards us, his face wild with a crazed delight, and as our eyes took him in, there was a surge forwards, and cries of disbelief. Abidan's face and hair, his clothes and skin, were dripping wet! 'Water!' he panted. 'We have water!'

We all crowded in, touching him, squeezing his robe and licking our palms. But my father quickly raised an authoritative hand bidding us to step back and calm down.

'Abidan, lead us to where God has provided.'

It was the strangest sight when we got to the rock. None of the usual signs, no plants or marks of a riverbed, yet water poured freely out of the ground. It was almost dark but nobody cared – we drank and washed and played in the water, even my solemn father splashed his feet like a child.

I wondered why I had ever thought that our young foolish adventures would save the day. But my mother had a surprise for me later. 'Thank God you sneaked off like that,' she said. 'The men were ready to kill Moses. They were calling on your father to lead them back to Egypt! The only thing that stalled him was not knowing where his children were.'

I watched again as my father cupped some water in his hands and threw it over my squealing sister. She came running to where I stood with my mother, shouting, 'See? God looks after us! Daddy always knew it!'

My father winced. But he also smiled.

Exodus 33:12–23

THE FACE OF GOD

A: It's you!

B: Of course it's me.

A: And how did I know it was you?

B: Because you know me, and you know *(pointing at own face)* this is me, the face you know so well!

A: Exactly! I know your face! It's unique! It's you!
      The face of *(B's name)* ... unmistakable!

B: All right, what's got into you? What's this all about?

A: What does God look like?

B: Uh?

A: Haven't you ever wondered? What does God look like?
       God's unmistakable face, what does it look like?

B: God doesn't *look* … anything. God can only look like … God!

A: Exactly! And what does God, looking like God, look like?
       Do you know, Moses once wanted to know what God looked like.
       I know how he felt.
       I mean, how can we know God is with us, if we don't see anything;
       if we don't see God's … face.

B: How can God have a face?!
       God doesn't have a face!
       What, you really think God has a face?

A: God's got a face all right, because God said to Moses,
       'you cannot see my face'.
       Then God walked past Moses and let Moses only see his back!

B: If God's got a face, why wouldn't Moses get to see it?
       Why don't we get to see it?
       You know, you're right,
       it would be pretty cool to see what God does actually look like.
       Yeah! What does God look like and when do we get to see?

A: If Moses had got a peek,
       he wouldn't have lived to tell the tale, apparently.
       I think I get what God was saying.
       Imagine seeing *all* of God, *all* at once,
       imagine what kind of a face that would be.

B: I don't think you could get one single face
       that could hold all of who God is.
       It would blow your mind!

A: Exactly! So how many faces would God need,
       so that we can handle what we see?

A little bit of God in this face and a little bit of God in that face? Maybe God thought, 'This is how I'll show them what I look like' ...

B: Uh-huh. Makes sense.
        Sooooo, where are all these kazillions of faces of God?

A: *(turning to look closely in growing wonder at B's face, pause)*
        Could be there's one right here.

A&B: *(slowly, in amazed, pensive tones, as though penny is dropping)*
        Made ... in the likeness ... of God!

        (Pause)

A: *(slow and emphatic)* I have *seen* the *glory*!

B: *(turning to look closely at A's face, pause)* Here's another one here.

A: Do you really think so?

B: *(slow and emphatic)* I have *seen* the *face* of God!

A: But, there are new faces all the time! Can there really be so much of God to see?

B: So much to see, so much to know, a never-ending mystery!

A&B: *(looking out, gazes spanning congregation's faces)* WOW!

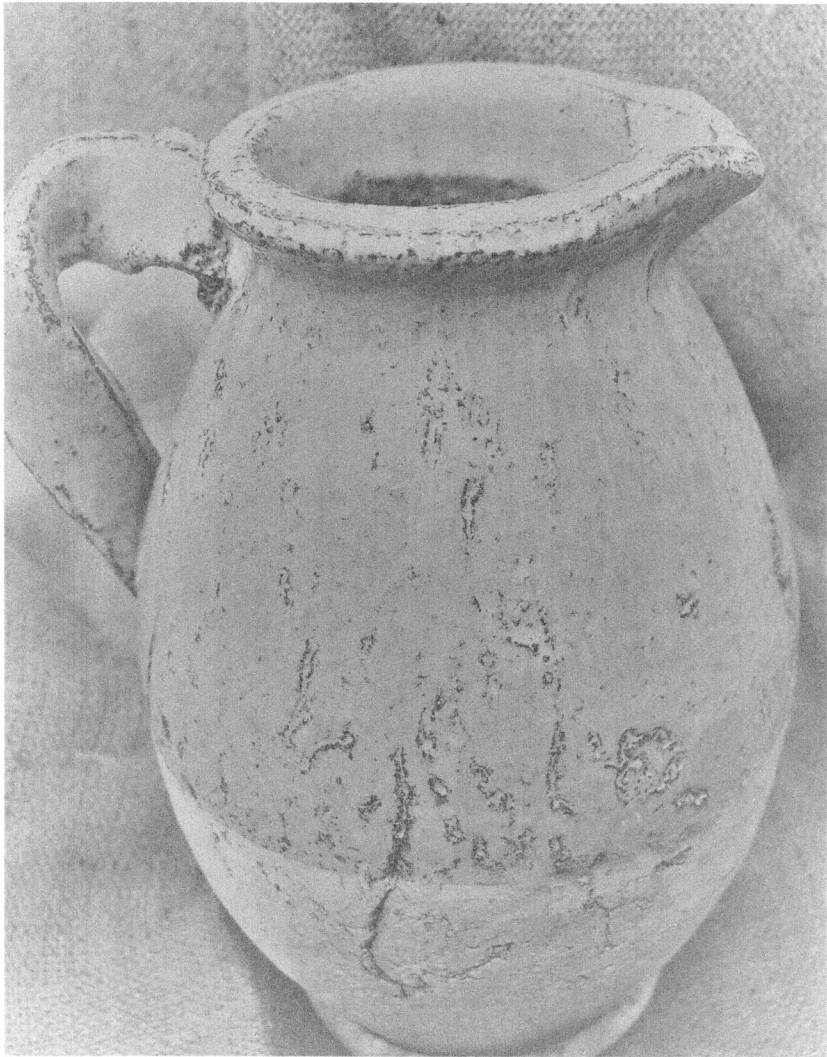

Numbers

Numbers 14:1–12

FEAR OR TRUST

A: Moaning, greeting, complaining, catastrophising.

B: Pleading, prostrating, reasoning, encouraging.

A: If only we could go back!

B: If only we could go onward!

A: Fearmongering, wailing, dreading, rebelling.

B: Calming, refuting, protesting, proclaiming.

A: We're going to die!

B: We're going to live!

A: We will be killed!

B: We will be protected!

A: Listening to the fear, imagining the worst.

B: Looking at the possible, willing to trust.

A: There's danger ahead!

B: There's safety ahead!

A: It's a terrible place!

B: It's a very good land!

A: Stop trying to persuade us!

B: Stop shouting us down!

A: Just take us back to how things used to be!

B: Just come on into the future God has for us!

A: Stuck again.

B: Stuck again.

A: Between fear

B: and trust.

MOSES' DIFFICULT DAY (YOUNGER RETELLING)

A long time ago, in the middle of a long journey between two countries, God's friend Moses had a very difficult day. He had been leading a huge crowd of people from a country where they had all been slaves, to a country that would be their new home, though they had never seen it before.

A few people had run ahead from the crowd to take a look at the new country. Was it safe or dangerous? Was there any food there? Were the people friendly or unfriendly? Would it really be a good new home or not?

Some people came back saying it was safe, but some said it was dangerous. Some said, 'Well, God has always looked after us, we'll be fine!' But some felt scared and said, 'Maybe we should go back to the country we used to live in!'

So everyone stopped and no one would take another step forward. A big argument started between all the people who felt scared and worried, and the small group with Moses – just him and three others called Aaron, Joshua and Caleb. The four of them kept saying that everything would be fine and they should keep on going.

'It's a wonderful place! God wants us to feel at home there! Come on, let's go!' said Caleb and Joshua and Aaron and Moses.

'Nooooo! We'll be picked on and we'll starve and we'll be miserable. Let's go back to where we were before!'

'But look how well God has looked after us already! God still cares. God will keep us safe!'

'Nooooo! It's a strange land. How can we know what will happen to us? We might get hurt or attacked!'

Even God got quite impatient. 'Will you all be scared forever? Will you ever really trust me?'

I wonder what we would have done if we were in the crowd that day. Would we have felt scared to go into the new country? Or would we have trusted that God would keep us safe? Or maybe a bit of both? What situations have made you feel scared to go somewhere, and what has helped you to feel safe?

DEUTERONOMY

Deuteronomy 34:1–12

Making it home

A dialogue between Moses and Joshua, as though up Mount Nebo. Moses needs to wear a long coat or suchlike, under which is hidden a relay baton.

Moses: Well, would you look at this! We've actually made it. We're back.

Joshua: Bit of a roundabout route, but what's forty years, eh!

Moses: Erm, four hundred and some, more like.

Joshua: Did it feel that long?!

Moses: No, I mean that's how long we've really been gone.
Before Egypt, before Pharaoh, before slavery, this was our home!
And we're finally back.

Joshua: Is that what kept you going? Imagining this place?

Moses: Ha! Let me tell you, I needed a lot more than that
to get me to get you lot here.
But yes, I did imagine this place …

Joshua: Can you see Abraham's old house from here?

Moses: Oh, ya daftie. How would I know? I'm not *that* old!

Joshua: We should find it though, and open it up as a museum!
After all that digging we did in the desert, we'll be great at
unearthing archaeological finds!
Abraham's crook, Jacob's old soup pots,
Esau's bow and arrow, the complete heritage centre.
We can bury you there, too, with a plaque, and should we plant
you an oak tree?

Moses: Joshua, we're not here to build shrines to the past.
(Wistfully, and almost to himself)
And you'll have more important things to do …

Joshua: But what you've achieved should stand for all time!
         People should know!

Moses: What people should know is that we got here together.
         I needed Zuar's encouragement and Elishama's wisdom.
         I needed Adina's shoulder to cry on, and Ofra's hot dinners!
         Whatever's been achieved, it's taken all of us.

Joshua: No, your part has outshone everyone's!

Moses: No, my part was I happened to pay attention to a burning bush.
         Many's the time I've wished I'd ignored it!
         The rest has been about all of us, together or not at all.
         Think about it, what's kept you going?
         Putting me on a pedestal,
         or your mother's stew and your cousins' games
         and Rina's prayer times and Joab teaching you to be a man?!

Joshua: *(after a pause, nodding slowly and chuckling)*
         OK, I see what you mean … you're right!
         But what have I done? What has my part been?

Moses: You know how a relay race goes, Joshua?

Joshua: *(puzzled)*
         Uh-huh …?

Moses: *(revealing baton and holding it out to Joshua)*
         It's your turn now. Trust God. Keep the vision alive.

Joshua: *(looks at the baton, takes it firmly and deliberately, looks back at Moses.
         They hold each other's gaze. Freeze.)*

JOSHUA

Joshua 3:7–17

NO GOING BACK

A pensive but deeply hopeful monologue by Joshua. Could be done with the Joshua reader standing alone, or with a group who join in with the italicised repeated words, in a quiet, low tone.

Getting out of the place that has held you captive …
entering into the place you truly belong …
either way, there's always a crossing over.

> *And when the sea opens up before you*
> *and closes in behind you,*
> *there's no going back.*

And the question is always:
What's on the other side?
Will the grass really be any greener?
Should you not just stay put
with the devils you know?

Moses led us from Egypt.
I had to lead us from the wilderness.
Two merciless places,
but they were home;
the only home ever known
to those leaving them behind.

> *But when the sea opens up before you*
> *and closes in behind you,*
> *there's no going back.*

We were still captives in the wilderness:
captives to our fears, our immaturity, our victim mentality.
Some of the complaining voices were only silenced by death.
We learned the hard way
about refusing to grow up
and move on.

But when the sea opens up before you
and closes in behind you,
there's no going back.

So, from a burning bush or a flooding river ...
different starting places, different paths ahead,
but for both of us,
yes, a crossing over
from where we've reached
to where we need to go next.

And when the sea opens up before you
and closes in behind you,
there's no going back.

Welcome home! ... to this strange land,
where everything has changed
and yet God is still with us.

For the sea opened up before us
and closed in behind us,
and praise God,
there's no going back!

Joshua 24:1–25

THE STONE AT SHECHEM

Monologue by a woman of the tribe of Dan.

Shechem.

I'm not here often these days,
so I couldn't resist looking for the oak tree,
and there it was,
still thriving after all this time.

The stone is still there too.
As soon as I saw it – oh the memories that came flooding back.

None of us knew it was the last time we would see Joshua.
The last time we would hear his great voice booming out at us.
Not calling us to battle; not proclaiming victory;
not telling us which tribe was to have what land.

The day here at Shechem called us to a far bigger picture.

We had all but forgotten!
We had lost sight of anything beyond tribal territory.
History and heritage had been obscured
by our obsessions with harvests and homemaking.
What did it matter where we came from and where we were going?
We were wrapped up in the daily grind
of food and family, and sometimes fighting.

I belong to the tribe of Dan.
Dan, not just a name we liked, not just a name we dreamt up.
Dan, one of the sons of Jacob.
Jacob the twin of Esau, the sons of Isaac.
Isaac the son of promise, the son of Abraham.

Why do we know these names?
Why should we remember these names?
Why care about these stories?

Why did Joshua take us back to the beginning and tell us all over again
about our ancestors,
about Egypt and Moses, about the desert and the mountaintops
and Canaan, with its battles
but also its grapes and olives
that we eat yet never planted?

Because this is how we know our God.
God who has breathed on us and blessed us from the beginning.
God who has woven grace and gift into our every step.
How could we know God's faithfulness
but by knowing the lives of Abraham and Isaac and Jacob;
of Moses and Joshua?
Yes, Joshua …
the new great hero we must never forget.

As for me, even in my own tribe my name is barely known.
A woman of the least of families.
But that day, here at Shechem,
was for me as much as any other …
for me to choose – will I serve the Lord?
Will I live in covenant
with the One who has given my people this promised land?
Will I look beyond the next meal,
see what life with the Lord God means?

I watched Joshua set up the stone and in my heart I was afraid …
but I cried YES!

JUDGES

Judges 16:4–31

PLAYING GAMES

Delilah, Delilah, look at this silver –
all yours if you tease out the truth from your lover.
What is his strength's secret? How well you'll be paid;
persuade him with whatever game can be played.

Delilah, Delilah, here's what to try –
seven fresh bowstrings that have not gone dry.
Bind him, subdue him, how well you'll be paid,
but the bowstrings don't bind him, what a game he has played.

Delilah, Delilah, here's what will subdue –
tie him with ropes that have never been used.
Hold him, control him, how well you'll be paid,
but the ropes don't restrain him, what a game he has played.

Delilah, Delilah, here's what to do –
weave the locks of his hair and pin to the loom.
Quell him, suppress him, how well you'll be paid,
but the loom doesn't lick him, what a game he has played.

Delilah, Delilah, here's what he said –
take a razor and shave every hair from his head.
Crush him, constrain him, how well you'll be paid,
by the razor he's revealed his foolish game played.

Samson, oh Samson, what have you done –
lies upon lies and then why your strength gone?
Outwitting, defeating, how well they'll be paid,
when the final act of your game is played.

SECRET STRENGTH (YOUNGER RETELLING)

Remember the strong man Samson? Do you remember what made him so strong? It was his long hair! That was the secret to his strength – he had never had a haircut! He once had a special friend called Delilah who was promised a lot of money from Samson's enemies if she could find out the secret of why he was so strong. They didn't know it was his long hair that did it. Delilah didn't know it was his long hair that did it. But she wanted the money, so she tried to find out.

So Delilah asked Samson, 'Samson, you're so strong! But how could your strength be beaten?' What do you think he told her?

'See that bow and arrow? Tie me up with brand-new strings from a bow that has never shot any arrows, and I'll lose my strength.' Was that the truth? Delilah waited till he fell asleep and then tied him up with brand-new bow strings that had never shot an arrow. What do you think happened? Samson broke free, as strong as ever. 'Whoaaaaaarrrr!'

Delilah asked again, 'Samson, you're so strong! But how could your strength be beaten?' What do you think he told her?

'See that rope? Tie me up with brand-new rope, and I'll lose my strength.' Was that the truth? Delilah waited till he fell asleep and then tied him up with brand-new rope. What do you think happened? Samson broke free, as strong as ever. 'Whoaaaaaarrrr!'

Delilah asked again, 'Samson, you're so strong! But how could your strength be beaten?' What do you think he told her?

'See that weaving loom? Braid my hair into the loom, and I'll lose my strength.' Was that the truth? Delilah waited till he fell asleep and then braided his hair into the weaving loom. What do you think happened? Samson broke free, as strong as ever. 'Whoaaaaaarrrr!'

Delilah asked again, 'Samson, you're so strong! But how could your strength be beaten?' What do you think he told her?

'See my long hair? Cut it all off, and I'll lose my strength.' Was that the truth? Delilah waited till he fell asleep and then cut off all his long hair. What do you think happened? Samson couldn't break free. His strength was gone.

'Aaaaaaaaarrrgh!'

I wonder why he told so many lies. What do you think about that? I wonder why he told the truth in the end. What do you think about that?

When Samson's enemies saw that his strength was gone, they made him their prisoner. They were really nasty to him and they even hurt his eyes so badly that he became blind. He was a prisoner for a very long time. But his enemies forgot about one thing. Can you guess what they forgot to do? They forgot to cut his hair! So it grew and it grew and it grew. And it made Samson get stronger and stronger and stronger. And one day he was led out to act like a clown for his enemies to laugh at. He couldn't see anything but he could feel the big stone pillars of the house where he stood. He put his hands against two pillars. He knew that he was now as strong as ever. 'Whoaaaaaarrrr!' The pillars broke and the house fell down on Samson and on all his enemies. And that is the end of the story.

RUTH

Ruth 3:1–18

FOR FUTURE SECURITY

You could invite people to group together in threes and to designate themselves Naomi, Boaz and Ruth, then to listen to the story from their given character's perspective. After hearing the story, invite people to have a short time of conversation in threes, sharing reflections on what each character might have been thinking and feeling as events unfolded.

A: Two widowed women in Bethlehem.

B: Naomi and Ruth.

A: Mother-in-law and daughter-in-law.

B: Israelite and Moabite.

A: One had arrived home.

B: One had arrived as a foreigner.

A: Their story became known around town.

B: The bitterness of Naomi with no grandchildren.

A: The loyalty of Ruth even with no children.

B: Their story became known to Boaz.

A: A relative of Naomi's.

B: Not her closest relative, but a good man.

A: Meeting Ruth, he proved himself trustworthy, kind, generous, protective.

B: Meeting Ruth, he saw her as honourable, faithful, hardworking, humble.

Both: WHAT NEXT?

(Pause)

A: The harvests were gathered.

B: It was time to thresh the grain.

A: A job for the men.

B: Thresh the barley then celebrate!

A: Eat, drink and be merry!

B: Sleep contentedly by the heap of grain.

       (Pause)

A: Naomi sent Ruth to the threshing floor.

B: In her best clothes and her sweetest perfume.

A: Washed.

B: Scented.

A: Beautiful.

B: Naomi sent Ruth to Boaz's bed.

A: In secret.

B: In stealth.

A: In darkness.

B: Naomi was seeking security for Ruth's future.

A: Ruth was willing to do as she was told.

B: Boaz was astonished to wake up and find a woman at his feet.

       (Pause)

A: Boaz promised to give Ruth the secure future she needed.

B: Ruth stayed beside him till morning, leaving before anyone saw her.

A: Naomi waited to see what would happen, confident that Boaz
       would keep his word.

Both: WHAT NEXT?

NAOMI'S PLAN (YOUNGER RETELLING)

Remember Ruth and Naomi? They came from Moab to Bethlehem together, hoping to be safe and happy. How sad they must have felt when their husbands died in Moab. Ruth's husband was Naomi's son, so poor Naomi had done a lot of crying for her husband and her sons, who were all gone. In those days, long ago, the best way for a woman to be happy was to marry a kind man and have children. But what if your husband died before you? What if you had no children, or your children died before you? Naomi felt too old to get married again and have more children. But how happy she would be to see Ruth get married again and have children! Naomi wondered if she could help Ruth to find a new husband.

In Bethlehem, Ruth and Naomi were cheered up by the kindness of Boaz, who let Ruth work in his fields, and made sure she was looked after well. Seeing how kind Boaz was, Naomi had an idea. One night, when Boaz had finished working, Naomi sent Ruth to the barn where Boaz was having his tea. What a hard day's work! Oh, how tired Boaz was! He finished eating and lay down and fell asleep. Zzzzzzzz … In the middle of the night, Boaz woke up suddenly. Who was there? Someone was beside him! Oh, it's Ruth! Boaz and Ruth sat up talking in the dark barn, and kind Boaz understood that Ruth had been sent by Naomi, and that Naomi was trying to look after Ruth by finding her a new husband. Boaz sent Ruth back to her own house, but first he promised her that everything was going to be fine. Naomi was very happy when she heard what Boaz had promised. 'Let's wait and see what happens now,' she said to Ruth, 'but we can be sure of this, my dear Ruth – everything is going to be fine!'

Ruth 4:1–22

SECURITY SEALED

A:　Boaz had promised security for Ruth's future.

B:　Naomi trusted him to keep his word.

Both: WHAT NEXT?

A:　Boaz called on the man who was Naomi's closest relative.

B:　And Boaz called on ten village elders too.

A:　Boaz told the closest relative about some land he could inherit.

B:　The land belonged to Naomi's late husband and her lost sons.

A:　'You are first in line to be given this land,' Boaz told the relative, adding …

B:　'If you don't want it, I am next in line to have it.'

A:　The relative said, 'Yes, I'll take the land.'

B:　'Then you'll take her daughter-in-law Ruth as your wife,' said Boaz.

A:　Hearing this, the man changed his mind.

B:　'No, I won't take the land then,' he said. 'You can have it, Boaz.'

A:　The village elders watched and listened.

B:　They saw Boaz take off his sandal.

A:　It was a sign of making an agreement about the land.

B:　The village elders were witnesses to the agreement.

A:　'The land now belongs to Boaz,' they agreed, adding …

B:　'And Boaz will marry Ruth.'

A: All the people who witnessed the agreement gave their blessing to Ruth and Boaz.

B: 'We hope you have a lovely family!' they said.

A: And very soon, Boaz and Ruth had a son.

B: The women called him Naomi's son.

A: The women called him Obed.

B: The women celebrated with Naomi
because she had a daughter-in-law
more loving and loyal than seven sons.

A: No more bitterness for Naomi.

B: No more barrenness for Ruth.

A: A widowed Moabite remarried to a good man.

B: A widowed Israelite with new life in her old age.

BOAZ'S PLAN (YOUNGER RETELLING)

Remember Boaz and Ruth and their midnight meeting, talking in the barn? Remember what Boaz promised? 'Everything will be fine!' he said. So what did he do next?

In the morning, Boaz went to sit at the village gate, which was always the place people met on important occasions. Boaz asked ten village leaders to sit with him and watch what he did next. He also asked the man who was the closest family member to Naomi's dead husband to come and listen to him carefully.

'Naomi has a field,' Boaz told the man. 'You can have this field, because you are the closest relative to Naomi.' The man thought he would like to have the field, until Boaz went on, 'If you take the field, you will also have to keep the field in Naomi's family name, and so marry her daughter-in-law Ruth.' The man thought about it and said to Boaz, 'I think it's best that you have the field, Boaz.' All the village leaders watched and listened as Boaz and the man made an agreement: that Boaz would have the field and he would also marry Ruth. Everyone wished Boaz and Ruth a happy marriage. 'We hope you have lots of children!' said all the women. So Boaz married Ruth and soon they had their first baby, a boy called Obed. Naomi was so happy to see that, just as Boaz had promised, everything was turning out fine.

SAMUEL

1 Samuel 3:1–21

First Encounters

An older Samuel looks back on his childhood encounter with God.

I remember the first time I ever heard God speak. I had never heard God's voice before. I didn't even really know God at all yet. It was when I was still young, living alongside my teacher Eli, who was so old and so wise in my young eyes. I looked up to him in every way. My mother had told me to serve the Lord with all my heart and to learn from Eli what it meant to be a priest, a prophet, God's servant.

I had fallen asleep in my usual night-time corner of the Temple, close to the Ark of God's presence. Something woke me in the middle of the night. Someone calling my name. I got up and ran to Eli, who came to at the sound of my footsteps and my asking, 'What is it? I'm here, sir!' But whatever I'd heard, it wasn't Eli. It all happened a second time, after I'd fallen asleep again – someone calling, 'Samuel! Samuel!' It made me nervous. If it wasn't Eli, then who was in the Temple and what did they want? Where was the voice coming from and why were they calling out to me, a child, and not my master the prophet? Why didn't Eli know who it was or why it was happening?

The third time, Eli had begun to think harder. He told me to give the calling voice an answer: to tell it I was listening, to let it say what it wanted to say. I had hardly pulled my blanket around me when the voice called for the fourth time. I sat up. 'Speak to me,' I said, and waited. 'I'm listening,' I said, not knowing what to expect.

Then I heard those terrible things, horrible things, about Eli not stopping his sons from saying awful things against God, and how Eli would be punished. My wise, beloved old teacher was going to be punished, and no sacrifice or offering would change God's mind. No one had heard God's voice so clearly in years and years … now here I was, a boy alone and burdened with these terrible words, lying in the dark, wide awake and terrified, clutching my blanket and blinking back tears, until dawn crept in. I wished I had never woken Eli. I wished he didn't know about the voice.

But of course he asked me, 'What did the Lord say?' I couldn't bear to answer, but he insisted that I be honest and spare him nothing. Did he somehow know or fear it was a word of judgement? Had he been carrying the shame of his sons' behaviour? Did he know that there would be a reckoning?

So I told him everything, fearing for what he might do when he heard it. But he did not tear his clothes or wail or cry. He did not beg for mercy or rush to make a sacrifice. He did not prostrate himself in prayer before the Ark. He was silent for a moment, then all he said was, 'It is the Lord. Let him do what seems good.' What seems good? I remember being astounded. Was this the God I had been told about but had never encountered? A God who called on children to deliver messages of destruction to prophets who just accepted it as good if God said so? I wasn't sure I wanted to hear from this God again. However, as you know, the Lord had other ideas …

GETTING THE MESSAGE (YOUNGER RETELLING)

Who knows best – a grown-up or a child? Who is the wisest – someone very old or someone very young? Who would God speak to if God had something important to say – someone aged 60 or someone aged six?

Grown-ups know more than children, right? Old people are wiser than young people, right? God would want to talk to a 60-year-old rather than a six-year-old, right?

Here's a story to think about. A long time ago, there was a very old man and a very young boy who worked together in God's Temple. The old man, Eli, was a priest, and the little boy, Samuel, was learning how to be a priest. Now, Eli had two sons who behaved very badly. Eli did nothing to stop them. God felt very unhappy about Eli's sons and when God saw that Eli did nothing to stop his sons from behaving so badly, God thought, 'I'm going to have to tell Eli how upset I am.'

God wanted to be sure Eli got the message. Eli was an old man. Eli was a wise man. But God didn't go and talk to Eli. God decided to talk to the little boy Samuel who worked with Eli in the Temple. Samuel had never heard God speaking before. But one night when Samuel was fast asleep in his bed, God gently called out his name and woke him up! At first Samuel thought it was Eli shouting for him. Eli thought Samuel must have been dreaming.

But God kept calling, 'Samuel! Samuel!' until at last Eli said, 'It must be God who is calling your name!' So Samuel listened to God and heard how upset God was about Eli's sons and their bad behaviour. Samuel was scared to tell Eli what God had said. It was a hard thing for Eli to hear. He really had let God down by not telling his sons that they needed to behave with more respect and kindness.

So Eli the priest listened to the little boy Samuel, and Eli understood that God doesn't always speak to a grown-up when something important needs to be said. God doesn't always choose to talk to an old person or a wise person. Sometimes children can be the best listeners, and the best hearers, even when it's a difficult message that God wants to pass on.

1 Samuel 8:4–11; 16–20

ASKING FOR A KING

The people said to Samuel,
'We really want a king!
Please find someone to lead us,
to fight for us and win!'

Samuel told the people,
'Here's what a king will do –
he'll send your sons to battle,
he'll make life hard for you!

'The best of everything you have
the king will make his own!
You'll have to work much harder,
and then you'll moan and groan!'

But the people said to Samuel,
'We want a king to reign –
like all the other countries!
We want to be the same!'

Samuel told the people,
'But we've got God above,

who only wants the best for us,
and leads and rules with love!'

But the people wouldn't listen,
'We want a king!' they said.
'What will I do, Lord?' Samuel cried.
God answered, 'Go ahead,

'give them what they ask for –
a king to rule them all.'
So Samuel searched the land
and chose a man called Saul.

What kind of king, I wonder,
did Saul turn out to be?
Did he make the people happy?
We'll have to wait and see …

1 Samuel 15:34–16:13

DAVID IS CHOSEN TO BE KING (YOUNGER RETELLING)

Have you ever done something that felt like a really good idea, but turned out to be a horrible mistake?

Remember the story about the people wanting a king? Samuel thought it was a bad idea. God thought it was a bad idea. But all the people thought it was a good idea. They wanted a king – they really wanted a king!

So finally God said, 'OK then.' And Samuel said, 'Here he is then. King Saul.'

Did everyone live happily ever after? Oh no! Oh dear! Saul wasn't very good at being a king. And God wished he had never made Saul the king!

So did God say, 'That's it! No more kings! They're a bad idea!'?
Did God say, 'I told you so!'?
Did God say, 'I knew this would happen!'?
Did God say, 'Well, didn't I warn you!'?
Did God say, 'See what happens when you don't listen!'?

No, he didn't. God is kinder and more patient than that. He knew the people still wanted to have a king. Even though it might not be the best idea. So God tried again. He asked Samuel to find a new king. This time it was a boy called David. He was the youngest in his family and he was very good at looking after sheep. What on earth made God think a young shepherd boy could be king? But that's who he chose. David.

What kind of king, I wonder, did David turn out to be?
Did he make the people happy? We'll have to wait and see …

1 Samuel 16:1–13

VOTED OUT!

Eliab: *(overjoyed)* It wasnae me! Yeeeesssssssssss!

Abinadab: *(extremely annoyed)* It *should* have been *me*.

Eliab: What are you talking about?
          It should never have been you!
          It *should* have been me, actually.

Abinadab: But you didn't *want* it to be you! And it *wasnae* you.
          So it should have been me!

Eliab: Why did you want it to be you?
          It's a lucky escape, bro, that wee eejit can have it –
          I'm glad it's him, and no' me!
          And no' you either!

Abinadab: But I wanted it! He'll be a right pain in the neck now.
          He'll think he's better than us.
          If you didnae get it, I'm the next in line, but no,
          all seven of us get passed right over for that wee nyaff.

Eliab: Away an' complain to Sam then. He's your man.
          It's all his doing.
          But I don't see why you're so bothered.
          Aye, thank God it wasnae me!

Abinadab: How come you didn't want it anyway?
How come you think it's a lucky escape?
That was your big chance for glory,
and you're glad to miss out?
How come?

Eliab: Aw, work it out, will you!
The king is still alive and well,
though rumoured to be going a bit nuts,
and good old prophet Sam anoints someone else
to be the next king.
Well, you bet I'm glad it's no' me
with the sign on my head saying 'king's rival'.
Just wait till word gets out –
I don't think our wee bro will last a minute.
He'll be hunted, for crying out loud!

Abinadab: But prophets aren't in the business of
putting people's lives in danger.

Eliab: Aye right!
What was the first thing Pharaoh did
when Moses went asking for liberation?

Abinadab: OK, OK, he doubled the workload of the slaves for a bit,
but it was all right after that.

Eliab: *(sarcastically)* All right after that?
Sure! Everything was just dandy, save for a few plagues,
a near drowning,
near death by thirst,
and near mutiny against the great prophet
for putting people's lives in near *constant* danger!

Abinadab: *(after a thoughtful pause)*
Do you really think wee Davy will be assassinated or something?

Eliab: How can we know?
What happens now, who can say?

Abinadab: So much for being the Lord's anointed.
No' much of a pleasure really.

Eliab: Nope.

Abinadab: But does it not put Sam on a dodgy footing too,
                 if the king finds out what he's done?

Eliab: Mhmm. Great perks and privileges, being a prophet.
                 Bet you wish that was you too?

Abinadab: Should you or Dad not just have
                 stopped all this happening then?

Eliab: Ah, and you'd like to do a better job
                 of being eldest son or father as well?!

Abinadab: I'm just thinking what all this could do to our family.
                 He's still our kid brother.

Eliab: And he's been anointed by a prophet
                 and chosen by God to be king.
                 You want to argue with that?

Abinadab: But I don't get it.

Eliab: Neither do I.
                 But what I do get is this –
                 you and I are still to be what we've always been.
                 Shepherds, soldiers, sons and brothers.
                 That's quite enough to live up to.

Abinadab: Do you think wee Davy actually wishes it wasnae him?

Eliab: Maybe we all live up to what's asked of us.
                 And he's no' that wee any more.
                 It might make him less of an eejit.

Abinadab
and Eliab: OOR DAVY FOR KING! GAUN YERSEL, WEE YIN!

1 Samuel 17:1; 4–11; 32–49

DAVID DEFEATS GOLIATH (YOUNGER RETELLING)

If you know the tune to the children's game 'The Farmer's in His Den', you can sing this! Pick someone to be David and let them act the part, with props if you wish!

Before wee Dave was king,
before wee Dave was king,
he went to fight a Philistine,
before wee Dave was king.

'I've fought with lions and bears,
I've fought with lions and bears,
where's the giant, I'm not scared.
I've fought with lions and bears!'

'Here, David, put these on,
here, David, put these on,
helmet, sword and armour strong.
Here, David, put these on!'

'This helmet hurts my head!
This helmet hurts my head!
I cannae wear this lump of lead!
This helmet hurts my head!

'This sword weighs a ton!
This sword weighs a ton!
I cannae pick it up and run!
This sword weighs a ton!

'This armour doesn't fit!
This armour doesn't fit!
I cannae even walk in it.
This armour doesn't fit!

'I'll take these stones and sling,
I'll take these stones and sling,
God will help your future king,
I'll take these stones and sling!'

2 Samuel 1:1, 17–27

SAUL AND JONATHAN KILLED IN BATTLE (YOUNGER RETELLING)

Do you have a best friend? What do best friends do for each other? Did you know that David had a best friend? His name was Jonathan and his Dad was Saul, who was king before David. Remember that Saul wasn't a very good king? But his son Jonathan was a very good best friend!

In those days, long ago, lots of young men were soldiers for the king. They had to go and fight in terrible battles. Today there are still soldiers who fight in wars. Can you imagine if your best friend had to go to war? David and Jonathan sometimes didn't even know if the other one was still alive.

One day a messenger came to David with some terrible news. Many soldiers had been killed that day. Saul and Jonathan had been caught in the midst of the fighting and they had both died.

Poor David! He was heartbroken. He couldn't believe his best friend was gone. He was so upset he ripped his clothes and just cried and cried. All of his other friends wept with him. It's really hard when sad things happen, especially when we lose someone we love. I wonder if you have ever felt like David did when Jonathan died. I wonder how we can help each other when someone feels their heart is broken.

2 Samuel 5:1–5, 9–10

DAVID'S CITY (YOUNGER RETELLING)

Have you ever noticed that the names of some places sound like names for a person? Let's see if we can think of any?

(St Andrews, Keith, Fort William, Colinsburgh, Leslie, Douglas, Johnstone, Angus, Peterhead, Crawford, Fraserburgh, Fort George, Barry, Irvine, Campbelltown, Neilston, Stewarton, Helensburgh …)

Imagine having a town or city named after you? Let's make up some imaginary place names with our names …

Remember David, whose life we've been learning about? After that sad time of losing Saul and Jonathan, David became the new king. Everybody wanted him to be their king, because he was a good leader and he was very brave. He made the city of Jerusalem his new capital city and he went to live there. Soon the city was given another name. It was called 'David's City'. That just shows how important David was, how famous he was, and how good a king the people thought he was.

2 Samuel 6:1–5, 12–19

HEAVEN TOUCHED EARTH

A monologue by an unnamed woman reflecting on the occasion of the Ark of the Covenant being brought to Jerusalem.

Heaven touched earth today! Or did we see how heaven is always among us, if we will only wake up to it? Of all the ways to see God … after all the fighting, all the battles, all the times we've heard him say slain soldiers are proof of the divine presence …

Where is God in the conflict, the conquests? They pray before drawing swords, yet still go out in fear and come back in grief, while we wait to hear who has been widowed this time.

But today was a day of peace. Peace far beyond the lack of armour. Peace … the sounds of laughter from our men, music in the streets, a great picnic in the city! A great swell of our brothers, fathers, husbands, one moving mass of noise and song, and all to bring the Ark of the Lord into the heart of this place, David's City.

And there he was, our king, whirling and shouting, leaping like a lamb, carefree as a child, abandoned to the celebration, caught up in the moment, and barely dressed! One of the people, one with his people!

Peace, perfect peace! If only it was that simple. When it's not the enemy out there, it's the enemy within.

Did anyone else see her, then, as I did? Frozen, aloof, at that high window. Haughty eyes and a cold stare, before she turned away and disappeared.

What held her back? What is her self-imposed imprisonment? How wonderful if she too had been down here among us, here where she belongs, with her royal husband and her devoted people.

Even when heaven touches earth, we find it so hard to let ourselves be loved.

DANCING WITH THE KING (YOUNGER RETELLING)

It's time for a party
in Jerusalem town!
The king is so happy
he's dancing around!

God's top ten rules
in a great big box
are coming to the city
where the party rocks!

> *Will you step with me*
> *for a one, two, three?*
> *Let's give it some kicks,*
> *for a four, five, six.*
> *Let's clap along in time*
> *for seven, eight, nine.*
> *And spin for the end,*
> *we're at number ten!*

There's a trumpet playing
and a tambourine,
everybody's hopping
like a jumping bean!

God's top ten rules
in a great big box
are coming to the city
where the party rocks!

> *Will you step with me …*

2 Samuel 7:1–14

Rewriting the plans

Nathan approaches David to break the news that God is not enthused about the ideas discussed the previous day. Nathan begins hesitantly and nervously.

Nathan: *(feigning lightheartedness)* Good morning, your majesty.

David: *(upbeat and a bit distracted)* Morning, Nath!

Nathan: Good night's sleep, sir?

David: No! I was wide awake all night – it was wonderful!
I've got so many ideas for the Lord's house!

Nathan: *(almost to himself)* I was afraid of that …

David: *(enthusiastically)* The best cedar, the finest gold …

Nathan: Erm … your majesty …

David: *(not really listening)* … a grand porch and pillars …

Nathan: But sir, there's just one problem …

David: *(really looking at Nathan for first time)* Problem, Nath?
Oh, look at you, didn't you get much sleep either?

Nathan: *(unhappily, hesitantly)* I was, erm, dreaming.

David: Dreaming! Yes! Isn't it wonderful to dream!
What did you dream for this house we're going to build?

Nathan: *(becoming bolder)* The Lord had something to say about that.

David: He did?! How amazing!
Well, what does he want?
Bronze? Copper? How many pillars?
Did he say how big the whole thing should be?

Nathan: *(confidently now)* His message wasn't quite along those lines,
your majesty.

David: Well, tell me then, Nath! What is the word from the Lord?

Nathan: *(calm and matter of fact)* He doesn't want a house.

David: *(shocked silence)*
            But ...
            We have to!
            We need a place, for the Lord to dwell!

Nathan: *(beginning to understand and warm to the alternative)*
            He doesn't want a house.
            God has lived with us and moved with us
            ever since our ancestors left Egypt,
            and has never asked that we build him a house.

David: But look at this house of mine –
            my refuge and my haven!
            I can't give God any less!

Nathan: I think that may be precisely where God sees things differently.

David: Now you've lost me.

Nathan: To build the Lord a house
            would be to give him less.
            We cannot put the Lord in any building, your majesty.
            Cedar and stone can never contain his presence.

David: *(pausing, and then arguing another angle)*
            But the people need a place to go,
            somewhere strong and solid and tangible,
            as a sure sign that God is with us.

Nathan: It would not take long
            for those static walls and fixed adornments
            to be seen as a 'sure sign'
            that God has settled down
            and is standing still.

David: *(disappointed)* But they would be so beautiful,
            the porch and the pillars ...

Nathan: ... Pillars of fire and cloud;
          the beauty of mountains, valleys, stars:
          this is how we have known the Lord.

David: But it seems such a wonderful dream.

Nathan: The Lord's dreams are far bigger than ours.
          The promise is that *God* will build *you* a house!

David: *(more excited, intrigued)* Not of wood and ore?

Nathan: Of body and spirit, your majesty!
          A *people* in which the Lord will live!
          Learning, loving, growing, moving on together!
          And your name – *David* – they will always speak of
          as a testimony to where they come from and who they are.

David: *(amazed and humbled)*
          Bless the Lord!
          May he build the house he deserves,
          and may we live up to our place in it.

DAVID AND THE HOUSE FOR GOD
(YOUNGER RETELLING)

Encourage the children to give their own ideas as the story unfolds. Whatever they think, accept and respect all contributions!

Remember King David, who we've been learning about? After David settled down in the big city of Jerusalem and people started calling it 'David's City', David had a big idea! Ping! He thought he should build a house for God. He thought God's house should be right in the middle of the city. 'After all,' David thought to himself, 'I've got a lovely big house for me and my family, so I think God should have a place to live in too! I'm going to build a house for God!' What kind of house do you think David was thinking of? ... What would it look like? ... How big would it be? ... What would David put inside it?

Do you think that building God a house was a good idea? ... Do you think God wanted a house to live in? ... What do you think God said to David about his idea? ...

It was a nice idea, but actually it wasn't what God wanted! Nope. Why do you think God didn't want a house? … Does God need a house? … If God doesn't need a house, then where does God live? …

Sometimes we call the church 'God's house' because it's a special place to pray and meet together and learn about God. But is this where God lives? It's good to remember that God lives everywhere, and we can be with God everywhere we go.

2 Samuel 9:1–13

MEPHIBOSHETH

In a style deliberately echoing the story of Tamar (Genesis 38:6–26). How does another disadvantaged individual, this time a disabled man, fare in a society that in all probability regarded him as cursed because of his disability? It could be interesting to compare the stories of Tamar and Mephibosheth and their respective routes to safety and security.

Mephibosheth. Son of the late Jonathan, beloved friend of the king.

Plan A – that Mephibosheth would grow up healthy and strong, a man in a world of men.

But a childhood accident left him lame for life, at the mercy of others' kindness.

Plan B – good news – a protector for Mephibosheth, 'dead dog' in an able-bodied world. Taken in by Machir, son of Ammiel, in Lodebar.

Plan C – even better news – the king desired to show goodness to any of his late friend Jonathan's surviving family. The disabled son given a permanent seat at the king's table. Blessed and well fed. The land belonging to his grandfather given back into his ownership. Compassion and protection through no effort of his own. Known and cared for because of who he was. No need for a survival plan. No need for risk or desperate measures.

Mephibosheth, adopted son of a forefather of Christ.

2 Samuel 11:1–15

BATHSHEBA'S AGONY

An emotion-charged dialogue between Bathsheba and the wife of Joab.

Jemimah: Bathsheba! There you are.

Bathsheba: Jemimah! Thank God you're here.

Jemimah: I've just heard the terrible news.

Bathsheba: It can't be worse than what I need to tell you.

Jemimah: Bathsheba –

Bathsheba: *(interrupting)* Listen, this is more important.
             Have you heard from Joab?
             Do you know if the men are coming home soon?

Jemimah: *(hesitant)* Coming home soon?
             You really haven't heard, have you?

Bathsheba: *(urgently)* Jem, I need to see Uriah!
             I mean, I need him to come home.
             I need him to … lie with me.

Jemimah: Lie with you?
             Don't you know what's happened?

Bathsheba: I know what's happened all right!
             I'm pregnant, Jem, and it isn't Uriah's baby.

Jemimah: *(accusatory)* What?
             He goes off fighting and you are with another man?

Bathsheba: *(indignant)* No!
             Jem, I need to see my husband,
             to cover up what has been done to me.

Jemimah: *(it's dawning on her what Bathsheba is talking about)*
             Done to you?

Then you should shame this man!
Who is he?
He should be stoned!

Bathsheba: No!
If Uriah comes home soon,
it will look like the child is his.

Jemimah: It's too late, Bathsheba …

Bathsheba: No, it's not too late, it's only been a month.

Jemimah: But … *(pausing, making sense of other things she knows)*
Uriah was sent home from duty one night last week.
Joab was puzzled, because the king insisted on it.

Bathsheba: The king sent him home?
So he thought of the same cover-up.
But Uriah didn't come to me.
So it didn't work.
Uriah is too honourable …

Jemimah: *(aghast)* You don't mean? …
Tell me you're not saying…

Bathsheba: Yes.
I am with the king's child.
Don't you see, I can do nothing against him?

Jemimah: *(distraught)* Oh no!
Now it all makes sense. Oh no, no …

Bathsheba: What is it?

Jemimah: When Uriah returned to duty,
Joab received the second message from the king.

Bathsheba: What message?

Jemimah: To put Uriah to the frontline,
to the heaviest fighting …

Bathsheba: No!
             Is he safe?
             Have you heard?

Jemimah: That's why I came to find you …

Bathsheba: *(trying not to hear the inevitable)* Why? Why did you come…?

Jemimah: I just heard … the terrible news …
             It's too late, Bathsheba …
             He has fallen, he is dead.

Bathsheba: *(utterly devastated)* Noooo!
             Uriah, Uriah …
             O God, help me …

DAVID AND BATHSHEBA (YOUNGER RETELLING)

This is a tough story but, as far as possible, we shouldn't shy away from it, even with children. I've focused on the issue of 'taking what isn't yours' but many children also know only too well the reality of betrayal in adult relationships, and how new partnerships can be forged under less than ideal circumstances. Accept whatever the children share of their own experiences, and their own sense of what God might say when we behave at our worst.

Today's story is not very nice. Sometimes people do things that are very hurtful and unkind. I wonder what things have happened to us that have made us feel upset, and sad, and angry. We've been hearing stories about King David, who did lots of good things and was a very good king. But he made some terrible mistakes too. Here's a story about one of the worst things he ever did. He took something that didn't belong to him. It was much worse than breaking someone's toys, much worse than stealing money, much worse even than breaking into a house and robbing someone.

It all started one day when he saw a lovely woman called Bathsheba. She was married to one of David's soldiers, a man called Uriah. But David didn't care how much Bathsheba and Uriah loved each other and how happy they were together. He decided that he wanted Bathsheba to come and live with him instead. And how do you think he made sure that he got what he wanted? What would he have to do to take someone's wife away from them? He made sure that the next time Uriah went into battle with the other soldiers, he was left alone against the enemy. So Uriah was killed, and it was really David's fault that he died. What a terrible thing to do to one of his loyal soldiers. What a terrible thing to do to Bathsheba.

I wonder how God felt about what David did. I wonder what God wanted to say to David …

KINGS

1 Kings 12:1–17, 25–29

STOLEN DREAMS

One of the older men reflects with great regret and bewilderment on Rehoboam's choice.

It was a chance for us all. A better future. An easing of our burdens. He came and asked for our advice! He came and sat down with us and listened. Here is a chance, I thought. Here is a real chance of a different way ahead. He heard what the people said. What courage he has, I thought, to hear his father criticised and to take it. No defensive knee-jerk reactions. No angry justifying of his father's policies. 'Lighten our load – will you lighten our load? – and we will serve you.' He heard us. Surely he saw what kind of leader he needed to be – a servant, whom we would gladly, loyally serve forever. Lighten our load. That's all we asked.

He asked for time. Time to think and to consider. This is a good sign, I thought. No arrogance. No haste. No presuming he automatically knew best. That's when he came to me. 'How do you advise me to answer the people?' He knows full well what I will advise, I thought, but he needs our backup. He wants a second opinion. Ah, he is still young, I thought, but this willingness to learn is a sign of wisdom.

I gathered those of us who had attended his father, those of us who had seen the years of hardship most keenly, those of us grown old and tired yet never despairing of a better day. He knew our love and loyalty to his father, in spite of the taxes and the labour demanded of us. We did not cast up all those past mistakes. We simply reinforced and reaffirmed what was needed now. Now, we need a leader who will serve, a servant who will lead. We need a king of gentle words, of compassionate policies. A king who knows how life is for the common workers. A king who will not beat us down but will lift us up.

And the more we talked, the more clearly we could see this future, imagine it, feel it coming. I felt my heart expand, I felt my breath quicken, something was stirring among us in that small gathering of souls. Surely he understands, I thought, he sees it too; he feels our confirmation of what he must say and do. He can lead us, he will lead us, into better times.

But he tore our hearts from within us. He trampled our dreams into dust and ripped away our vision. Just when we could see so clearly all that might have been, he turned away and rejected our plea. He chose to make our load heavier, our lives harder, discipline without kindness and labour without compassion. Why? What love can there be now? What loyalty? What future?

You could follow this up with a short time of shared conversation or quiet thought, inviting people to consider why Rehoboam, and indeed any leader, would make the choice he did. Why would any person in power choose to govern harshly rather than win people's loyalty through servant leadership?

WHAT SHOULD THE KING DO? (YOUNGER RETELLING)

A long time ago there was a new king who needed some advice. He was called Rehoboam, but let's called him King Reb for short. The people in his country were feeling pretty tired and upset. Their last king, who was called Solomon, had made everyone work far too hard, and had made them have to survive on not much money too, because he took so much tax money away from them. Everyone hoped that Reb would be much fairer than Solomon. Everyone hoped that Reb would be a kinder king and make life a bit easier, so they could work hard but not get so tired, and pay their taxes, but still have enough money to live on.

Reb decided to ask some friends for advice about how he should treat his people. How should he behave? Should he be kinder and fairer than Solomon, or should he be just the same, or maybe even tougher? He asked some old friends, and he asked some young friends. Before we find out what his friends said, imagine Reb came to us for advice. What would you tell him to do?

(Spend time discussing this. What would the children say to Reb? Why should he be fairer? Why should he be tougher? What might make him decide one way or the other?)

Well, Reb's older friends said, 'Reb! The best thing to do is be fair and kind to people. Then they'll like having you as king and they'll do what you want, because you're good to them.'

But Reb's younger friends said, 'Reb! The best thing to do is to be even tougher than Solomon! Make them work harder and show them you're in charge – you're the king!'

Who do you think Reb listened to?

(Discuss this and see what the children think.)

Well, Reb decided to listen to his younger friends, and he told everyone he was going to get tough and they were going to have to work twice as hard! It was a very bad choice to make. For the people in Reb's country, life was never the same again. They had hoped things were about to get better, but King Reb made things worse.

1 Kings 17:1–24

RAVENS ABOVE!

His God told him I could feed him.
His God sent him to me.
Me! A woman with nothing.
A woman convinced her next meal would be her last.
A widow expecting to die of starvation.
What a great choice his God made – picking me!
A hungry stranger sent to me!

And he asked me for bread.
What was I supposed to do?
I had no bread!
And pitiful little flour and oil to make any.
How terrible to have to tell a stranger that you can't feed them.
Never in my life have I had to say no.
Well, I couldn't bring myself to say it quite that bluntly.
After a lifetime priding myself on welcoming strangers
and feeding anyone who came to my door,
now my last act on earth was going to be a refusal to look after this man.
Ah, you might say, but what does hospitality matter
when you're about to die?

That's the thing – it mattered a lot!
Was I about to die in shame as well as in hunger?

I told him I was going home to use the last of my flour and oil
for my son and myself.
I thought the man would understand.
I thought he might say some word of release or blessing from his God,
that I would be forgiven for failing in my duty to him.

Instead he said I should bake for him first, then for me and my son!
I laughed and I groaned, but it got worse.
He made wild claims that my oil and flour would never run out
until the rains came.
Was he already so hungry he was losing his mind, the poor soul?
I just nodded and went off home.
In a daze, I went through the motions,
pour the flour, pour the oil, knead the dough,
all the time watching my son, praying.
What would it matter to have endless bread,
what would it matter to see this stranger fed,
if I lost my boy?

I wondered if his God heard me,
if his God was cruel.
The wild claims about the oil and flour came true –
we had food enough, I don't know how.
I was astounded and grateful beyond words,
but just as all seemed well,
my boy began to slip away, fevered and breathless.
Why? Why give me hope then snatch it away?
Why not let us die together in hunger but at least in peace?
Why send a stranger to my door who brings such trouble?

Yet he shared my agony, this man.
He questioned his God.
The man cared about my son, not merely his own stomach.
He made no more wild claims of miraculous happenings,
he just stayed by my son and cried to his God.
I could not bear to be in the room.

When the crying stopped, my heart stopped.
I waited for him to come down and tell me what I dreaded to hear.
But then I heard another cry.
Weak but familiar
and calling for me!
My dearest boy!

Was this man a prophet then?
A man of God, surely!
All he said was he had once been saved from starving by wild birds,
so it was not so hard to trust me!
Strange the things that give us faith.

THE BIRDS AND THE BREAD (YOUNGER RETELLING)

A long, long time ago, one of God's friends, a man called Elijah, was feeling lonely and sad and hungry. God wanted to look after him and cheer him up, so he sent some wild birds to fly around Elijah and drop food for him to eat. The big black ravens came to the ravine where Elijah was sheltering, in the morning and again at night, dropping pieces of food for him to eat. But God knew that the ravens couldn't keep feeding Elijah forever, so he told Elijah to get up and go to a nearby village. There was a woman there called Emuna who was feeling lonely and sad and hungry too. Maybe, thought God, Emuna and Elijah could help each other.

'Excuse me, kind lady,' said Elijah. 'Could you give me some bread?'

'I'm so sorry, I've got no bread left,' said Emuna. She felt very sad that she couldn't help Elijah. 'I'm on my way home to see my son and bake my last loaf with my last little bit of flour and oil. I don't think we'll stay alive much longer, we are starving.'

But Elijah had a funny feeling that Emuna could help him. Surely God had sent him to the village to find a friend and find some food. So he pleaded, 'Please could you bake some bread for me first? Then you and your son can have some.'

Emuna was surprised but she wanted to help, even though her own son was hungry too. She was even more surprised when Elijah said, 'Your flour and oil won't run out just yet. You'll see!'

Emuna walked home, puzzled but excited. 'My flour and oil won't run out? Why did he say that? Of course they'll run out! I've got so little left in the jars. Oh dear! What can I do? I really want to help that poor man, but I've nothing to give him! But he says my flour and oil won't run out?'

Emuna got home and began to make dough for the bread. She poured a little flour. She poured a little oil. She mixed the dough. Surely that was the flour and oil finished. She tipped up the flour jar again. Out came more flour. 'Oh! Look at that!' cried Emuna. She tipped up the oil jar again. Out came more oil. 'Oh! Look at this!' cried Emuna. She would be able to make enough bread for Elijah and for her son and for herself after all! Nobody was going to go hungry. She kindly invited Elijah into her house and gave him some bread. Oh what tasty bread! Elijah and the woman didn't feel hungry any more. They didn't feel sad any more. They didn't feel lonely any more. Elijah felt glad that the birds had fed him and that Emuna had baked bread for him. Emuna felt glad that her flour and oil jars still weren't empty and that her visitor was someone special. Elijah and Emuna were glad they had been able to help each other, just as God thought they could.

1 Kings 17:8–24

THE JAR AND THE JUG

Elijah monologue

Women, foreigners, children! Keep them out of sight, out of the way, out of the equation. We know they exist, we know our duty of care, but we keep them … at a distance.

That worked pretty well for me, until a week ago. Ugh! I came face to face with them – a starving Phoenician widow at death's door and her sickly fatherless infant. And I was reduced to throwing myself at her mercy! I've never been so humiliated – me, crying out to a foreign woman for food and drink!

Ask me to take on kings, God, I'll do it! Ask me to take your word to the city streets, I'll do it! But why ask me to be a guest in a house with empty shelves and a frightened woman at death's door?

Her jar and her jug, her meal and oil, they were running out. Running out. Every day as she tipped the jar and poured the jug, the meal and oil were running out.

And her son's vitality, the sparkle in his tiny eyes, the breath in his body, were running out. The woman did not care for your manna in her desert, Lord, she could do nothing but clutch her child and rock him, and when her gaze was torn from him to me, her rage and grief accused me of the boy's decline.

Ask me to warn the faithless of their fate, God, I'll do it! Ask me to witness the demise of the arrogant, I'll do it! But why ask me to bear the weeping of a poor mother about to lose all she has left?

When had I ever touched the dead, Lord? When had I ever embraced a child? When had I ever blamed you and begged you in equal measure and in such desperation?

Women, foreigners, children. Keep them in your sight. Widowed Melita and her little boy Hiram. Keep them in your sight.

THE WIDOW AND HER SON (YOUNGER RETELLING)

A long time ago, there was a little boy who lived with his Mum. They were both feeling very hungry. All their neighbours were feeling very hungry too. Nobody had had a proper dinner for days. There was a famine in their country – there was hardly any food left for anyone to eat. Mum went to her shelf and took her jar of meal and her jug of oil. She looked inside. There was only a handful of meal and a dribble of oil left. 'Oh no,' thought Mum, 'this will be the last cake I can bake, then we're going to starve!'

She went outside to gather firewood. She met a strange man who asked her for food. So she brought him back to her house and she lit the fire and baked the cake, and gave it to her visitor. She watched him eat it. The little boy watched him eat it. They were so hungry! But they wanted to be nice to their visitor. He was a man called Elijah, and he promised them that God would look after Mum and her little boy. Mum picked up her son and hugged him. She could see that he was getting very ill.

'Oh dear. Maybe I can scrape a little more meal from the bottom of the jar and squeeze a few drops of oil from the bottom of the jug, and give my child something to eat.' She picked up the jar and shook it hard. Out poured enough meal to bake another cake! She picked up the jug and turned it upside down. Out poured enough oil to mix with the meal!

And as long as the strange visitor stayed in the house, the jar and the jug kept pouring out meal and oil, and Mum kept baking cakes. They weren't hungry any more!

But she wasn't happy. Her son was not getting better. In fact, he was getting worse. Mum began to feel suspicious of Elijah, her strange visitor. 'Is it you who is making the meal and the oil keep pouring? Is it you who is making my son ill? You said God would look after us, but look at my son, he's going to die!' she cried.

Elijah didn't know what to say. And when the little boy died, Elijah didn't know what to do. He cried and he prayed and he asked God, 'Why? This woman has been kind to me, why has this terrible thing happened?'

God listened to Elijah's prayer. The little boy opened his eyes and sat up, wide awake and alive again!

1 Kings 18:20–39

PLAYING WITH FIRE

A reflection through the eyes of a prophet of Baal. How might the 'losing side' have told the story?

There were 450 of us and one of him. And he decided to take us on. It all started with his shouting, goading us, accusing us of limping along, unable to make up our minds about who is most powerful in this land. He wanted to push us off the fence and choose – his God or our God, his truth or our truth? Contests like that have no winners. What was he trying to prove?

How foolish we were to let him get under our skin with his irritating jeers. My God is bigger than your God. So he wanted it settled? Whose God is better? Whose truth is right? Fine, let's settle it: a quick showdown should give him the showing up he deserves. He wanted fire, he wanted a freak show. How foolish we were to start dancing to his tune.

He mocked us but we were making a mockery of ourselves. We were turning our own devotion into a crazed and desperate frenzy. Why would Baal deliver fire on cue for this foreign heckler? What was this game of gods supposed to achieve? Why were we competing for some hollow sense of supremacy? There were 450 of us and yet, alone, his aggravating little presence had us hooked and sucked right in. And the longer it went on, the more humiliated we became, and our anger against him rose. What would it take to stop this absurd argument, to halt it in its tracks? Why did we not cease our hysteria, sit down and see the pointlessness of this power game? But he was pushing our buttons hard and we were driven to saving face.

Of course there was no fire. We were defeated but still that was not his moment of claiming victory. He carried on to an ever more bizarre spectacle, pouring water on the wood until it ran like a moat, and then screaming out with one long shout to whoever he believed was there. And with a sudden crack, the altar he had built caught fire! The heat of it scorched our faces and terrified our minds and we cried our allegiance in the face of the flames. Then he believed he had won. Then he believed that settled it. He goaded us to a fight we didn't ask for and delivered a spectacle that brought no lasting change. What was he trying to do? And where did he go?

MINE IS BETTER! (YOUNGER RETELLING)

It was Tuesday evening so Katie went to Sports Club as usual. She noticed a new boy was there, visiting the club. Nobody had met him before. Katie thought maybe he wanted to join the club, but he wasn't really talking to anyone; he just wandered round and watched everybody. Katie joined four of her friends doing stretches and warming up for the running track. They were going to time each other to run one lap, to see if anyone was faster than last week. Mike and Ellie and Adi were trying out what they were learning about their long jump technique. Little Rebekah and Niko were using beanbags to practise their throwing and catching. And the new boy was just walking around, carefully watching.

All of a sudden, there was a loud shout. Katie was just about to start her running lap, but she stopped and looked up. 'Come here, everyone!' It was the new boy. 'Come over here!' he shouted again. Katie and her friends looked puzzled, but they went over to where the boy was standing.

'I go to a Sports Club just ten minutes away from here,' he began, 'and you should all come. It's much better than this! Let me show you what I can do! Who wants to time me if I run round your track?' Katie looked at him. He didn't look as fit as her. He wasn't as tall as Russ, and Russ was the best runner in the club. Russ stepped forward. 'OK, I'll time you.' The new boy leapt onto the track and took off as Russ watched the seconds tick by. Katie and the others watched the boy run, and then watched Russ's face, and then watched the boy run. 'Oh boy, he's fast!' thought Katie. Nobody needed to ask if he'd beaten Russ's best time. The new boy knew it too. 'See?' he said breathlessly when he got back to them. 'That's what I've learned at my Sports Club! Now do you want to see how good my long jump is?' Mike and Ellie and Adi all just stared at the ground. They had a feeling what would happen if they said 'yes' but they didn't want to be rude and say 'no'. Ellie mumbled, 'I … I think I have to go home early today. I better go. Bye everyone.' She turned and walked away. Katie felt awkward and went running off to catch up with her. They walked round the corner into the next street in silence. Then Ellie asked Katie, 'He was right, wasn't he? I bet he's good at all the sports we do. His club must be much better than ours.' Katie had to agree. 'I can't believe he could run that fast! Better than Russ!' They were quiet again, knowing they were thinking the same thing. 'Are you going to swap clubs then?' Katie asked Ellie. Ellie shook her head. 'What about you, Katie?' Katie shook her head too. 'No, I don't think I want to,' she said, 'even if it is better than ours.'

You could have a chat about Ellie and Katie's decision. Why do you think they didn't want to join the other Sports Club? What would you have done?

1 Kings 18:20–39

A FIERY CONTEST

A reading for all ages of the congregation to join in. You could print the full script on your service sheet, show the words on a screen, or have a 'leader voice' for the people in a cantor and echo style. To make the effect of the fire at the end, have two small groups of people at the front who sit or stand as the two piles of 'wood'. Baal's group stand still, unmoved! Elijah's group should have rolled-up strips of red crêpe paper hidden in their fists. When Elijah calls 'Light the fire' they can jump up and release the red paper, waving it around! Or concoct your own version of a dramatic finale!

King Ahab: I call on all the people of Israel and all the prophets of Baal to meet at Mount Carmel! Elijah has something to say.

Elijah: Will you lot make up your minds?
If the Lord is God, worship the Lord;
but if Baal is God, worship Baal!
None of the Lord's prophets are left except me,
but there are still hundreds of prophets of Baal.
Let's see who is the true God!
Let the prophets of Baal take a bull and put it on a bonfire –
but don't light it.
I will take another bull and do the same.
Then we will all pray to the god we trust –
let's see which god lights the bonfire!

All: **Yes! Let's do it!**
Here is the wood. Here is the bull.
Here is our bonfire, ready for Baal!
Come on, Baal! Light the fire!

Come on, Baal! Light the fire!

Elijah: I don't see anything happening.

All: **Come on, Baal! Light the fire!**
           Come on, Baal! Light the fire!

Elijah: My oh my, Baal really likes to keep you guessing, doesn't he?

All: **Come on, Baal! Light the fire!**
           Come on, Baal! Light the fire!

Elijah: Nope, no sign of a spark yet.
           Not to worry, there's no hurry is there?

All: **Come on, Baal! Light the fire!**
           Come on, Baal! Light the fire!

Elijah: Try shouting a bit louder, will that work?
           Is Baal away daydreaming? Has he gone to the bathroom?

All: **Come on, Baal! Light the fire!**
           Come on, Baal! Light the fire!

Elijah: You'd better pray harder!
           It looks like Baal has gone on holiday!
           Or is it just his day off?

All: **Come on, Baal! Light the fire!**
           Come on, Baal! Light the fire!

Elijah: I don't think he can hear you!
           Is he having a nap?
           Can't you wake him up!

All: **Come on, Baal! Light the fire!**
           Come on, Baal! Light the fire!

Elijah: Oh dear me! Let's see if God can do any better.
           Come and see what I'm doing.
           Look, I'm putting twelve stones in a circle,
           for the twelve tribes of Israel.

And I'm digging a deep trench around the stones.
Here's the wood, and here's the bull on top. Now watch!
I'm pouring gallons of water on the wood.
And again, lots more water.
And again, even more water.
The trench is full! The wood is soaking wet!
Now, O God, please prove it to us that you are the only God.
Show us that you are calling us back to you! Light the fire!

All: **The Lord is God! The Lord alone is God!
The Lord is God! The Lord alone is God!**

2 Kings 5:1–14

CURING THE COMMANDER

A dialogue for immediately before the Bible reading.

A: How To Cure An Army Commander.
Send him to the best doctor in the land!

B: Nope. That won't work.

A: It won't? What should he do then?

B: First, he'll have to listen to his wife.

A: Why? What will she know?

B: She will have been listening.

A: Ah! His wife will have consulted the best doctor in the land?

B: Nope. She will have listened to a little girl.

A: A little girl? Must be a very special little girl then.
Is she the daughter of the best doctor in the land?

B: No, she's just the servant of the wife of the Army Commander.
Well, a prisoner of war, to be precise. And a foreigner.

A: A young, female, foreign slave?! What will she know?!

B: She will know about a prophet.

A: Ah! The best prophet in the land?

B: No. The best prophet in a foreign land,
      the land she was captured from.

A: Wait a minute.
      In order to be cured, this Army Commander will be expected
      to take notice of the word
      of a young, foreign, female servant, via his wife,
      who will persuade him there might be
      a far-off, foreign prophet who can help?

B: Yes, we're getting there.

A: Huh, great plan so far.
      Right, he'll have to go to the king then,
      if a trip into foreign territory is required.

B: Nope. That won't work. Not that it will stop him trying.

A: But there's protocol for these matters!
      He'll need the king to give him a letter, which he will give
      to the foreign king, requesting the said cure,
      and surely, taking along a load of impressive gifts
      to ingratiate himself.

B: None of that will work. In fact it will make things worse.

A: What on earth will make things better then?

B: The prophet will hear about it.

A: Ah! The impressive gifts will be diverted to the prophet
      and he'll be persuaded to make an appearance?

B: Nope. The prophet won't care for any gifts.
      He won't even feel the need to show up.
      He'll just send a message.

A: What message? 'I will come and perform the ceremony of healing this time tomorrow'?

B: Nope. Just 'send the man to me'.

A: And you think the Army Commander
will go meet a prophet
he knows nothing about,
on the word of a lowly messenger, without any idea so far
about how he's actually going to be cured?
Will he not be vowing by now to never listen to his wife again?

B: He might. But he'll go along anyway.

A: Ah! And finally he'll be rewarded?
The foreign prophet will perform a wonderful ceremony of healing?

B: Nope. He'll just send out another messenger.

A: Another lousy messenger?!
Will these guys not know who they're dealing with?
He's an Army Commander, a man of power and prestige!
He deserves some respect!

B: They won't care much for power and prestige.
So yep, he'll take it as pretty disrespectful, which is a pity,
as it will be a fantastic message …

A: What will the message be? What will be so fantastic about it?

B: How To Cure An Army Commander. Final step.
He should wash seven times in the River Jordan.

A: No way! What an insult!

B: Unfortunately, that's what he'll say too.

A: I don't blame him! So will he get cured or not?

B: Oh yes, he'll get cured.

A: Ah! Will the prophet come up with a better Final Step?

B: Nope. A bunch of servants will dare to suggest
      it might be worth trying the seven washes.

A: Servants? More servants?
      After all that, this Army Commander
      is going to listen
      to a bunch of servants?
      Listening to a servant was what started all this nonsense!
      Will he not be screaming by now: 'Will somebody just cure me?!'

B: He might. But he'll do it.

A: And ......?

(Lead into Bible reading)

HEALING HELPERS (YOUNGER RETELLING)

As each person who did something to help Naaman get well is named, have a child come forward and wear the name of the person, so that you end up with every child playing a part in the story – have as many servants as needed!

A long time ago a man called Naaman was sick. He had leprosy. The leprosy made his skin sore and then it made his fingers and toes numb. Poor Naaman. This is the story about how he got well again. He didn't just get well all by himself. It took lots of help from lots of people to make him well. Let's begin at the end of the story and see how many people helped so that in the end Naaman got well. The one thing that eventually made Naaman's skin recover was when he went into a river for a bath. But who told him to go into the river? A *servant* brought him the message. But who sent the servant? *Elisha* the prophet did. And who really encouraged Naaman to have a go at washing in the river, just like Elisha advised him? All of Naaman's *servants* did. But how did Elisha get to know that Naaman needed help? He heard it from the *King of Israel*. And how did the King of Israel know that Naaman needed help? He heard it from the *King of Syria*. And why did Naaman go to the King of Syria? Because his *wife* said that the King of Syria would ask the King of Israel and the King of Israel would ask Elisha the prophet to cure Naaman. But how did his wife know about Elisha the prophet? She heard it from a *little girl* who came from Israel and had been captured in a war and brought to Naaman's house to be a servant. She told Naaman's wife, and Naaman's wife told Naaman, and Naaman asked the King of Israel, and the King of Israel asked the King of Syria, and Elisha heard from the King of Syria, and Elisha sent a servant, and Elisha's servant said, 'Go and wash in the river!' And all Naaman's servants cheered him on, 'Yes, sir, go and wash in the river!' And when Naaman went and washed in the river, he got better!

2 Kings 22:1–10

Unearthing

A dialogue, to follow the Bible reading, between the High Priest Hilkiah and one of the builders who has repaired the house of the Lord.

Hilkiah: What a transformation!

Builder: Thank you, sir!

Hilkiah: I knew you were the man to lead the restoration work.

Builder: Thank you … thank you, sir.

Hilkiah: When I think of the ruins you started with …

Builder: Yes, it didn't look promising. But I had a good team.
           And we know our materials.

Hilkiah: You do, you certainly do.
           Who'd have thought that simple wood and stone
           could be turned to this wonderful finish.

Builder: We reused a lot of what was here, sir.
           I can account for everything else, everything we had to buy.

Hilkiah: No, no, I told you, the king needs no accounts from you.
           Your honesty is beyond doubt.

Builder: Thank you, sir, and I'm honoured that his majesty thinks so.

Hilkiah: Did you come to his reading of the book you found?

Builder: The book *you* found! I only told you it was there.

Hilkiah: That's what I wanted to ask – how did you know it was there?

Builder: Like I said, sir, workmen know their materials.
            I knew it was neither wood nor stone I'd tripped on!
            It was something softer, under all the dust …

Hilkiah: Softer? *(Chuckling)* There is not much that is soft in God's Law!
            Did you hear the king's reading?

Builder: Oh, I heard it read the first time.
            When Shaphan first read it out to you, remember?

Hilkiah: You were listening?

Builder: Not at first, not really, except that I was curious,
            having been the one who … unearthed it.
            By the time Shaphan was five minutes into it, well,
            we had all downed tools …

Hilkiah: Really…? *(Pause)*

Builder: And all I could think was *(voice trailing off, shaking head)* …

Hilkiah: What? What were you thinking?

Builder: How was it lost? How did that happen?
            Did people get careless or self-assured or what?
            How did something so important get buried in the dust?

Hilkiah: We won't lose it again – that's for sure!

Builder: Such faith, sir, you have such faith.
            That's why you're the priest and I'm just a builder!

Hilkiah: *Just* a builder? You build, you restore, you transform.
            Look at this place!

Builder: I can do that for the Lord's house, sir,

but not for the Lord's people.
I don't know, I have a feeling we could so easily
bury all our best intentions all over again.
Forget how we're supposed to live.
Lose sight of God's commandments.

Hilkiah: Well, you know what to do then …

Builder: Do I?

Hilkiah: Just keep unearthing them …

REMEMBERING THE RULES (YOUNGER RETELLING)

One Tuesday after school, Laura said to her mum, 'Ask me again about the school rules, Mum!' Laura had been learning the rules her teacher wanted everyone to follow in class. Every day, she loved reporting back to her Mum about how well she was keeping the rules. So far this term, Laura was really proud of keeping the first three rules. It was the last one that was the hardest!

'OK,' said Mum that Tuesday. 'Tell me the school rules, dear.'

Laura screwed up her face as she concentrated. Then she repeated from memory the sign on the classroom wall. 'Arrive on time. Say please and thank you. Always try your best. And the number one rule for everyone, everywhere – treat others the way you want them to treat you.'

'And how did you get on today?' asked Mum.

'I was on time this morning! And I said please every single time I asked for something – to borrow Natalie's pencil sharpener, for David to fill up my water bottle at lunch, oh, and to take turns with Aswad on the skipping ropes at gym. I said thank you to the dinner ladies for my soup and sandwich, and to the janitor for helping us take the recycling bins out. And I tried my best at most things, Mum. Mr Johnston said he could see I was putting in more effort at skipping today. I'm getting better!'

'And how did you get on with the number one rule for everyone, everywhere?'

Laura sighed. 'Oh Mum! Treat other people the way you want them to treat you. That should be so easy! Why is it so hard? – it's hard to even remember that rule, then it's hard to do! I saw Kirsty sitting on her own at lunchtime and I didn't ask her to play with us. I would have wanted someone to ask me to play with them if I was sitting on my own, but I didn't do that for Kirsty. Why is it so hard?'

Mum sighed too. 'Laura, I wish I knew! You're right, we all forget very easily.'

Laura was surprised to hear her Mum say that even grown-ups found it hard to follow the number one rule for everyone, everywhere. Treat other people the way you want them to treat you.

'What can we do then, Mum?'

'Let's just keep reminding each other, will we? Because then we'll have the best chance of doing the right thing and not always forgetting. I think it's a rule we just need to keep seeing and reading and saying and hearing, over and over again! I know I need to be told more than once – I need to hear it lots of times – treat other people the way you want them to treat you! That's something I never want to forget.'

'Thanks, Mum, you're the best!' said Laura.

Have a chat with the children, asking what they thought of what Laura's mum said. Are there some rules that are good to hear lots of times, over and over again, whatever age we are?

JOB

Job 38:25–27; 41:1–8; 42:1–6

WORLD OF ANSWERS?

So,
what if there was
an answer for everything?
What if it all made sense?
What if everything could be explained?
What if everything could be understood?
What if there were no mysteries?
Nothing unresolved.
Nothing lacking closure.
Nothing left hanging.
Nothing to puzzle over.
Nothing beyond our control.
What if every 'why' had a clear 'because'?
What if there was an end to wondering?
What if all matters could be settled?
What if all lines of enquiry returned all necessary evidence?
What if we could get it all covered?
All worked out.
All neat and tidy.
No ragged edges.
No unfinished business.
What if we could find a place for everything
and keep everything in its place?
No anomalies.
No contradictions.
No paradoxes.
No ambiguities.
What if every single question
could be answered?
What if all fears could be tamed,
all monsters turned into pets,
and the rain never again fell on wasteland
or watered the wilderness?
What if we had that world?
Would we want it?

QUESTIONS WITH NO ANSWERS (YOUNGER RETELLING)

'I like asking questions!' said Luke to his friends one day.

'Me too!' said Penny. 'I like asking questions that nobody can answer!'

'Sometimes if I have a big question, I ask my Mum,' said Luke, 'and I'll say, but why, Mum? Why? And sometimes she says, "Just because." And I say, but that's not an answer, Mum!'

Penny and the others all giggled. They had all heard people say, 'Just because' when you tried to ask why. 'It means they don't know the answer!' laughed Paul.

'Let's think of all the questions we've tried to ask, that nobody could answer.' said Luke.

That got everyone thinking. Here are some of the questions Luke and his friends had asked that nobody could answer ...

When birds stop flapping their wings, why do they not fall out of the sky?

Why does the sky never run out of rain?

Why can you sometimes see the moon in daytime? And why can you never see the sun at night?

Why can't doctors make everyone who gets ill, get better?

What is there at the edges of outer space?

When we die, will we meet people who died before us?

Who made God?

Are some things that happen just pointless and meaningless?

How come no two people are exactly the same?

What questions would you add? I wonder what it would be like if every question could be answered. How do you feel about there being some things we'll never know and never quite understand? What's your favourite mysterious thing about the world?

Job 42:7–17

No longer the same

An unnamed friend muses on changes they see in Job.

Something's changed. What am I saying? Everything's changed! When you lose it all – the people you held dear, the possessions you treasured, the health you took for granted – it's gone forever. So his body is well again. His wealth is restored. His family has grown. But that doesn't bring back the past. That doesn't mean life is the same as it was; normality has returned. Far from it.

You'd think people would be talking about how doubly blessed he is these days. More head of cattle and sheep than ever before. More camels and donkeys than anyone who's lived. Yes, he seems happy again, joyous even. But that's not the most surprising thing. He's been throwing great feasts for his brothers and sisters and they've all brought him silver and gold with their sympathy and comfort for all he endured.

But that's not the gossip that's going round. No, what's set the neighbourhood buzzing are his new inheritance plans. The man who came so close to death has changed his mind about who will receive a portion of his estate. He's instructed equal shares be given to his daughters – equal to his sons!

Why would he do that? And to make no mistake, they are named – those names he chose for the beauty he sees in them – the Dove, Jemima; the Sweet-scented Oil, Keziah; the Radiant Eye, Keren-Happuch. Something's changed. He's not the same person. How could he be? But of all the ways to be affected by his ordeals, this is the strangest. Giving his daughters an inheritance? Why? What is he trying to say? After all his complaints that God cannot be fathomed!

HAPPY EVER AFTER? (YOUNGER RETELLING)

When you get to the end of a story, what usually happens? Do you like it when there's a happy ending? What stories do you know where everyone lives happily ever after?

Think of a few examples of happy endings – in films, books, fairy tales …

Is there always a happy ending? What else might happen? I wonder what kind of ending there is to the story in the Bible about the old man Job. Poor Job, what terrible things happened to him. His children died. His animals died. He became so ill he nearly died himself. He lost everything. Then his best friends tried to say it was all his own fault! They thought Job must have done something wrong, and that God was teaching him a lesson! Poor Job. He knew he hadn't been bad. He didn't understand why all these terrible things were happening to him. He questioned God. But all that God would say was, 'You don't know everything, Job.' And Job had to agree. 'You're right, God, I don't know everything.'

So could Job's story have a happy ending? What kind of happy ending could there be? Or maybe Job didn't live happily ever after. What do you think?

Ask the children for ideas about different endings to the story of Job. Which one seems most likely?

The story goes that, in the end, God gave Job twice as many good things as he had lost – twice as much money, twice as many animals, and even a new family, with sons and daughters to love. And Job lived for many more years, free from illness and sadness.

Do you think that's a good ending? Is that what real life is like?

Let the children reflect on this. You might want to say a short prayer for people who go through difficult times and don't get a happy ending.

Psalms

Psalm 8

HOW AMAZING!

A long time ago, there was a king who was wondering.
He was wondering about God.
He was wondering: just how do people find out how amazing God is?
It's not that God's a show-off!
It's not that God shouts out to us, 'Look at me! Am I not the best?!'
It's not that God jumps out at us, all dazzling and incredible!

The king in his wondering
went outside one night,
one very very dark night,
and he looked up at the sky –
there was so much light!
When the moon went down,
there were so many stars;
stars up here, stars over there,
hundreds of them, no thousands of them!

And even though the king knew he was quite an important person,
suddenly he felt very very small,
because the sky was so huge
and the night was so dark,
and the stars were so many!

But when he felt small, he also felt safe!
So very safe and loved and looked after.
'Wow!' thought the king,
'God made this huge sky, this dark night, these thousands of stars,
and God still sees tiny little me, and God never forgets me!
Now I know how people find out how amazing God is!
You just have to look at what God does,
especially on a very very dark night,
when God amazingly makes so much light!'

Psalm 23

WHAT A WEEK

Should be read reflectively with substantial pauses and real feeling. Could pre-cede or follow Psalm 23. Feel free to change 'events' of the story to better suit who and where you are.

What a week.

Wednesday. Biopsy result. I have never been so scared. Courage? Stoicism? No chance. Nothing but sheer terror. A black hole. I thought I'd be strong but I fell right in. Until you came and took my hand and pulled me through.

Thursday. Lunchtime walk in the park. In a daze. Until you stopped me, sat me down, showed me a few things. Daffodils blooming everywhere. Yellow heads nodding twice over in the pond's perfect reflections. Lush green grass growing back no matter how often it's trampled on …

Friday. Deep breath. The long-awaited and long-dreaded dinner with Brian. Sure enough, nothing but bitterness and bile. Until the waitress 'acciden-tally' brought two spoons with my ice cream. What had you told her? Life's too short.

Saturday. Aromatherapy massage at last, or so I thought, thanks to Julie and Pam's birthday voucher. Turned out a huge surprise – a whole spa day for the three of us! I felt spoiled rotten! By them. And by you. You don't bless us by halves.

Sunday. Your welcome on a sea of faces. Belonging made real in hugs and conversation. Something deeply good that I didn't have to chase after. There is nothing more I could ask for.

JENNY'S BRILLIANT DAY (YOUNGER RETELLING)

'Mum!' Jenny was excited as she jumped out of the car. 'Mum, wait till I tell you what a brilliant day I had!' Mum and Jenny went into the kitchen and Mum put juice and biscuits on the table. 'So you had a nice day with Gran?' 'Mum, it was the BEST day!' Jenny was too happy to even notice the juice and biscuits. She didn't even wait for Mum to ask what she'd been up to.

She just started telling the story of her brilliant day.

'Well, this morning we took Bruno for a big long walk. I know he's still a puppy, but his legs are getting so long already! We went to the park and I threw his ball a million times and he chased it and ran around for ages, with me running around playing with him. I ended up so thirsty and hungry, but Gran had secretly put my favourite juice and crisps and fruit in my rucksack – she's the best! And there was a peanut butter and jam sandwich too, and you know Gran doesn't like peanut butter, but she got some for me. Then I went on the swing and Gran pushed me really high! I could see the tops of the trees by the pond. I felt like a bird flying up there! Bruno was so funny, he ran around the swing in circles, then when I got off, he was so tired he flopped on the grass and let me lie down and put my head on him like a pillow! We went up into the woods after that, and it got a bit dull and rainy for a bit. I didn't like how dark it felt under the trees, but Gran held my hand and sang a silly song and made me laugh, so I stopped being scared. On the way back to the car we bumped into Tina and her Mum, and you know how she was so horrible to me at school last week? Well, she came up and said "Sorry, Jen!" and gave me some of her M&Ms. She said I was so lucky to go for walks with Bruno, and to have such a funny Gran. But I know Gran is more than funny, she cares a lot too, because in the car she was asking me what I've been doing and she just loves listening, and you know what she's like, she always tells me that she prays and asks God to keep me safe and happy and well. And guess what, back at her place, she had a banana loaf ready to go in the oven, so we played Snakes and Ladders while it was baking. I was sliding down every snake there was, and Gran said, "Let's make it a reverse game. I'll race you back to square one!" Then we had hot chocolate and hot banana loaf. Yum! So you see, Mum, it's just been the best day ever!'

Jenny looked at Mum and tilted her head, thinking. Then she said, 'Mum, do you think God cares about me as much as Gran does? As much as you do?'

Mum smiled. 'I *know* that God loves and cares for you *even more* than Gran does, *even more* than I do!' Jenny eyes widened. 'Awesome!'

Psalm 23

THE HOST AND SHEPHERD SPEAKS

You are my beloved lamb, my child, my dear one.
You belong to me like a sheep belongs to its shepherd.
I will see to it that you do not want for anything.
When you get tired, I will coax you into lying down
in lush green pastures;
when you are anxious and restless, I will lead you beside still waters;
when you feel depleted and defeated, I will restore the fire in your soul.
If you go walking into places that do you no good,
I will be true to my good name for leading you in the right paths.
Even if you walk through the darkest and bleakest of circumstances,
there will be nothing you need be frightened of,
because I will never leave your side;
like a shepherd with his rod to protect and defend,
and his staff to guide and lift up,
I will be there to fend off danger and draw you close to me.

You are my invited guest and I am your banquet host.
I will lay a table before you and prepare a hearty meal
where you can eat in fellowship with those who were your enemies;
I will bring oil and anoint your head as a sign of blessing;
your cup of wine will be full to overflowing.
Have no doubt that you will know my goodness and mercy
all the days of your life,
and you will belong in my house and at my table,
cherished in my sight and in my affection,
your whole life long.

RUNNING OVER (YOUNGER RETELLING)

Can be sung to the well-known tune 'Running Over'.

1.   Like a shepherd, like a shepherd,
      God is with me like a shepherd,
      knowing God loves me,
      I'm as happy as can be,
      God is with me like a shepherd.

2.   By the river, by the river,
      resting, playing by the river,
      knowing God loves me,
      I'm as happy as can be,
      resting, playing by the river.

3.   On the pathway, on the pathway,
      God will lead me on the pathway,
      knowing God loves me,
      I'm as happy as can be,
      God will lead me on the pathway,

4.   Nothing's scary, nothing's scary,
      in the darkness, nothing's scary,
      knowing God loves me,
      I'm as happy as can be,
      in the darkness, nothing's scary.

5.   Running over, running over,
      my cup's full and running over,
      knowing God loves me,
      I'm as happy as can be,
      my cup's full and running over.

6.   Safe and sheltered, safe and sheltered,
      in God's house I'm safe and sheltered,
      knowing God loves me,
      I'm as happy as can be,
      in God's house I'm safe and sheltered.

Psalm 27:1–6

IN THE SHADOW OF GOD'S PRESENCE

This monologue could be followed or preceded by a brief conversation or longer discussion in threes or fours, for example by inviting people to 'Share an experience you've had of God's presence being a real strength in the midst of difficult circumstances.'

I hear they're out to get me. They want to pull me down and they want me to know it. Hate is a strong word, but not too strong a word for this. I can't believe it's escalated so fast. One disagreement, one difference of opinion, and the whole situation spirals out of control. But I'm not afraid. God knows the truth and that's the light I'll walk by. What more could they do to me? They could still make things a lot worse. Stir up all kinds of lies and paint me as the real enemy. Yes, it hurts. It hurts when people you thought had more sense are actually taken in by the vicious rumours. I've never felt so aware of the power of evil. There's no other word for it. Could any of them take it further? Is my life in danger as I walk the streets? Should I stay behind closed doors, out of sight? What if there's someone angry enough, vengeful enough, to attack me? What would I want to do to someone if I believed what they believe about me? But do I really have need to fear? God is my strength and what a strength that is! I will live my life as I always have. Let them do their worst. Let them plan my ultimate downfall. The criminal record will be theirs, not mine. The only place I'm going to hide is in the shadow of God's presence. But I won't be cowering there – no, I will be singing!

Psalm 27:1–6

GOD IS LIKE A LIGHT FOR ME (YOUNGER RETELLING)

A simplified and rhyming version of the psalm, which the children could learn and make up actions for. Have fun explaining how 'round and round the clock' means 'all the time'. You could follow up by asking when they have felt like this themselves, and sharing some stories.

     God is like a light for me.
     I am not afraid!
     God is looking after me:
     I'm going to be OK!

If anyone is bad to me,
God will still be near.
If people try to hurt me,
God will still be here.

     God is like a light for me.
     I am not afraid!
     God is looking after me:
     I'm going to be OK!

When everyone's against me,
when everything goes wrong,
God keeps on loving me,
and so I'll sing this song.

     God is like a light for me.
     I am not afraid!
     God is looking after me:
     I'm going to be OK!

God is like a hidey-hole!
God is like a rock!
God is watching over me
round and round the clock!

     God is like a light for me.
     I am not afraid!
     God is looking after me:
     I'm going to be OK!

Psalm 29

THE VOICE OF GOD

Have you ever heard God's voice?
What do you think it sounds like?
What do you think happens when God speaks?
In the Bible there's a poem someone wrote long ago,
a poem about God's voice.
Here's what they thought …

> God's voice is like thunder – like a big booming drum!
> God's voice is like the rushing of a waterfall!
> God's voice is like the flashing of lightning!
> God's voice is like the sound of a huge tree trunk cracking!
> God's voice is like the wind whistling through leafy branches!
> When God has something to say,
> the earth shivers and shakes!
> When God speaks,
> he gives us strength and peace!

What do you think God's voice is like?
What kind of poem could we write?

Psalm 69:1–16

In our darkest moments

Psalms as songs and prayers, which cover the whole spectrum of human emotion, show us that someone else has been there before us and that God has heard. Doubt, despair, lament ... Do we pray like this? What do we do in our darkest moments?

Have you been there? Right down there in the pit? What do you do when you're going down and you can't stop? When you're up to your neck in it. When you can't take any more. If anyone looks at you, they won't think much of God. Haven't you been the one forever declaring God is good, yet your life is falling apart. You can't go on. There's nothing solid to hold on to. You've lost it; lost your grip; lost your ability to take so much as one more step. You're done in with trying; at the end of your rope after too much strife for too long. There's only so much one person can take and you've taken an overload. Nobody comes to ease the strain. You're an embarrassment, estranged from those you used to trust. The rest don't care, or worse, they mock you, look down on you, make you a spectacle, a butt for cheap jokes. How did you get here? How did life get to this? You don't even know any more. It's like being pulled down into sinking sand that sucks away your every last ounce of energy. It's like being swept off your feet by floodwaters that rush at you and threaten to drown you in their merciless surge. It's like falling into a swamp and thrashing around helplessly because there's nowhere to find a foothold and get out. It's like gasping for air one last time before the blackness swallows you whole. What do you do? How easily you could let the dark have you. No more tears and swollen eyes and aching throat. No more mockery and misery. What do you do? Do you still hope, still cling, still survive another wave crashing, still cry to God? What do you cry, and what good does it do? What if there's no answer? What do you do?

GOD, WILL YOU HELP ME? (YOUNGER RETELLING)

A simplified and rhyming version of the psalm, which the children could learn and make up actions for. You could follow up by asking when we have felt like this ourselves, and sharing some stories.

It feels like I'm sinking.
I don't want to drown.
It's like muddy deep water
pulling me down.

> *God, will you help me?*
> *I'm scared and I'm sad.*
> *Please put a stop*
> *to everything bad.*

Everyone hates me –
they're making up lies
and trying to hurt me –
it's making me cry.

> *God, will you help me?*
> *I'm scared and I'm sad.*
> *Please put a stop*
> *to everything bad.*

Something got stolen
and I got the blame.
Now everyone's laughing
and calling me names.

> *God, will you help me?*
> *I'm scared and I'm sad.*
> *Please put a stop*
> *to everything bad.*

ISAIAH

Isaiah 6:1–8

TOUCHED BY FIRE

I don't remember a face, exactly, but I know I was held in the gaze of God. What I saw first was a throne – a throne so majestic it could only be for God. Then there was the robe – a flowing, living robe – tumbling from the throne as if the Lord had just taken that seat of honour and spread that kingly garment like an endless train of purple satin, cascading down the steps like a rippling river of glory.

It was more than a seeing. I *felt* the presence of the throne, the robe, and around them the swirling smoke, and in the midst of the smoke I saw the wings of angels. Wings beating; wings hiding their faces from me; wings shielding me from the full revelation. Lord! My God! The words were in my mouth but I could not say a thing. The sudden presence of heavenly voices, so pure as their chorus rose. I can hear them yet, vividly, yet soundless. They penetrated the air, singing, 'Holy! Holy!' A cry and a conviction that overwhelmed me. Holy! I stood in the presence of a glory that filled the earth, beyond the throne and robe and smoke and wings! Holy! No sooner had I thought this than one of them came swooping down, bearing a hot coal outstretched to me, touching my lips.

No words, no need for words, but a wholeness within, making me fit to speak, to sing, to bear witness to God. Here I am, Lord. Yours – with an undivided heart.

A STRANGE AND SPECIAL DAY (YOUNGER RETELLING)

A long, long time ago, there lived a man called Isaiah who was one of God's friends. God had a special job for Isaiah to do and God wanted to tell Isaiah about it in a really special way. What happened was this – Isaiah had a vision! That meant he saw things that were not really there. But it wasn't like a dream when you're asleep and it wasn't that Isaiah was daydreaming and making things up. It was God's way of telling him something. First of all, Isaiah saw a big throne and it looked like a King was sitting there. The King was wearing a long, long robe. The air all around the King was full of smoky mist and in the mist, angels were flying! Isaiah thought the King and the throne and the angels were wonderful! He knew he wasn't dreaming. And he knew there wasn't really a King sitting in front of him. He knew it was all a big picture God was showing him. Then Isaiah saw one of the angels fly to him and touch his mouth with a piece of coal. Then the King asked, 'Who will use their mouth to tell people what I want to say to them? Who will speak for me? Who will be my friend?' What do you think Isaiah said? He said, 'I'll tell people what you want to tell them, God! I'll be your friend! You can send me to do that special job!'

It was all a bit strange and quite wonderful, but Isaiah wasn't scared. He was very, very happy!

Isaiah 7:10–16

GOD GIVES A SIGN

Two voices setting the stories of Ahaz and Joseph alongside each other, and showing how the same message spoke to them both, centuries apart.

A: Several centuries before the birth of Jesus,
B: Several months before the birth of Jesus,

A: Threatened by the powers of neighbouring kings,
B: Threatened by the discovery of a bewildering secret,

A: Ahaz, King of Judah, was afraid.
B: Joseph, carpenter in Judea, was afraid.

A: 'What am I going to do?' thought Ahaz.
      'My enemies are on the attack!'

B: 'What am I going to do?' thought Joseph.
      'My fiancée is pregnant and we're not yet together.'

A: 'But I will not put the Lord to the test,' thought Ahaz.
B: 'But I will not expose Mary to public disgrace,' thought Joseph.

A: The word of the Lord came to Ahaz from a prophet called Isaiah.
B: The word of the Lord came to Joseph from an angel in a dream.

A: And the message from the prophet said God would give Ahaz a sign.

B: And the message from the angel said God would give Joseph a sign.

A: This was the sign:

B: This was the sign:

A&B: 'LOOK! THE YOUNG WOMAN WILL CONCEIVE AND BEAR A SON AND SHALL NAME HIM EMMANUEL, WHICH MEANS, "GOD IS WITH US".'

A: This was the sign to bring courage and hope to Ahaz.

B: This was the sign to bring courage and hope to Joseph.

A: And Ahaz knew that the lands of his enemies would soon be deserted.

B: And Joseph knew that he should take his beloved Mary to be his wife.

A: In the stories of the ancient kings,

B: In the stories of the first Christmas,

A&B: EMMANUEL! GOD IS WITH US!

AHAZ AND JOSEPH (YOUNGER RETELLING)

A long, long time ago there was a king called Ahaz who was feeling very frightened. He was feeling frightened because of the two kings in the lands nearby. They were called Rezin and Pekah and they were getting ready to fight against Ahaz. Rezin and Pekah went out marching with their armies and began to attack a city in the land where Ahaz was king. Oh no! What if Rezin and Pekah's soldiers were strong? What if their armies were big? What if they smashed up the city? Ahaz was worried and scared and upset.

Could anyone help him? Yes, but it wasn't a soldier or an army or a fighter. It was Isaiah the prophet, a man who listened very carefully to God and told people what God was saying. Isaiah heard what God had to say, and he came to tell Ahaz. Isaiah said there was nothing to be afraid of. Nothing to be worried about. Nothing to be scared about. Nothing to feel upset over. Isaiah told Ahaz to wait and watch. Not for some extra soldiers to come along. Not for a bigger army to go out marching. Not for more people to defend the city.

'Wait and watch,' said Isaiah. 'Wait and watch for the most lovely thing, the most ordinary thing, the most special thing to happen. A woman is going to have a baby soon. It will be a baby boy. And before that little boy is old enough to start walking and talking and eating solid food, you can be sure that Rezin and Pekah with all their soldiers will have gone away. That is God's promise.'

For years and years after that, kings and mums and children and prophets told each other the story about Ahaz and the attacking armies and God's promise that they would be gone before a newborn baby grew up. One of the people who heard the story was called Joseph. Like Ahaz, he was feeling frightened too. He wasn't a king. He wasn't a soldier. He wasn't a prophet. He was just Joseph. And he was feeling frightened and worried about becoming a dad for the very first time!

One night when Joseph was sleeping, he saw an angel in his dreams, and the angel told him not to be scared, and that his baby would be a boy called Jesus. When Joseph woke up, he felt much happier about soon becoming a dad, and I wonder if he remembered the story about Ahaz, and I wonder if he maybe said a prayer, saying, 'Thank you, God. Long ago you looked after Ahaz. Now you're looking after me!'

Isaiah 9:2–7

SHEPHERDS PART ONE

Reader: Hear the words of the prophet Isaiah.

Shepherd 1: Bring it on.

Shepherd 2: We're all ears.

Reader: The people who walked in darkness …

Shepherd 1: That's us! Out in the night, every night.

Reader: The people who walked in darkness
              have seen a great light;

Shepherd 2: Huh – just the moon, occasionally.

Reader: those who lived in a land of deep darkness …

Shepherd 1: That's us again!

Reader: on them light has shined.

Shepherd 2: Just the moon and the stars.

Reader: You have multiplied the nation, you have increased its joy;
               they rejoice before you as with joy at the harvest,
               as people exult when dividing plunder.

Shepherd 1: Dividing plunder?
               What plunder do we get to divide, eh?

Shepherd 2: Carving up one of the flock when the wolf gets it.

Shepherd 1: If the wolf leaves us any …

Reader: For the yoke of their burden,
               and the bar across their shoulders,
               the rod of their oppressor,
               you have broken as on the day of Midian.

Shepherd 1: We've got *lambs* across our shoulders.

Shepherd 2: Which are *not* a burden.

Shepherd 1: And we don't want our rods broken.

Shepherd 2: They're all we've got to protect us.

Reader: For all the boots of the tramping warriors
               and all the garments rolled in blood
               shall be burned as fuel for the fire.

Shepherd 1: Fuel for the fire? Well, that sounds all right.

Shepherd 2: We like a nice fire to keep us warm in the night.

Reader: For a child has been born for us; a son given to us …

Shepherd 1: We much prefer lambs being born.

Shepherd 2: Daughter lambs even more than son lambs.

Reader: … authority rests upon his shoulders;

Shepherd 2: Like we said, we'll stick with shouldering lambs.

Reader: And he is named Wonderful Counsellor, Mighty God,
Everlasting Father, Prince of Peace.

Shepherd 2: Why not just 'Jimmy'…?

Reader: His authority shall grow continually,
and there shall be endless peace for the throne of David
and his kingdom.

Shepherds: DAVID!

Shepherd 2: We know about him.

Shepherd 1: He was one of us!

Reader: He will establish and uphold the kingdom of David
with justice and with righteousness.

Shepherd 1: Big words. What do they mean for us?

Shepherd 2: We're still a bit in the dark …

SHEPHERDS PART TWO

Shepherd 1: The people who walked in darkness

Shepherd 2: have seen a great light!

Shepherds: THAT'S US!

Shepherd 2: More than the moon!

Shepherd 1: More than the stars!

Shepherds: ANGELS!

Shepherd 2: Hundreds of them!

Shepherd 1: They came to *us*!

Shepherd 2: They shone on *us*!

Shepherd 1: Us – the old ones.

Shepherd 2: The rough ones.

Shepherd 1: Not the kings.

Shepherd 2: Not the priests.

Shepherd 1: Not the congregation.

Shepherd 2: Us – the smelly ones.

Shepherd 1: The invisible ones.

Shepherd 2: Not in the temple.

Shepherd 1: Not in the synagogue.

Shepherd 2: Outside, in the night.

Shepherd 1: Outside, on the edge …

Shepherd 2: … where you'd least expect them.

Shepherd 1: Not in the middle of worship.

Shepherd 2: But right in the middle of our work.

Shepherd 1: Not while we were praying or obeying laws
or making a sacrifice.

Shepherd 2: Just as we were doing what we do.

Shepherd 1: Not while we were hearing the scriptures
or singing the Psalms.

Shepherd 2: Not while we were thinking holy thoughts. *(Both laugh.)*

Shepherd 1: Just the usual, 'It's cold'

Shepherd 2: and 'Where's my blanket?'

   (Pause)

Shepherds: ANGELS ...

Shepherd 1: for a baby,

Shepherd 2: the wee lamb ...

Shepherds: AND FOR *US*!

Isaiah 35:1–10

TEN DAYS TILL CHRISTMAS

This needs plenty of oomph and energy in delivery! You could have the same voice for the repeated line, one or more other voices for the rest. Consider giving advance warning that the congregation can call out their own cries at the end; give folk a short time to think of or jot down a one-liner. Or compose a few lines for the readers to finish off the piece, with contemporary concerns and hopes.

Ten days till Christmas and the prophet cries:
   Water in the wilderness,
   blossoming land,
   springs for the thirsty ground,
   pools for burning sand!

Ten days till Christmas and the prophet cries:
   Dry lands rejoicing,
   the desert flowers,
   beautiful as fertile fields,
   see God's power!

Ten days till Christmas and the prophet cries:
   A path for God's people,
   no going astray,
   all danger and sadness
   chased away!

Ten days till Christmas and the prophet cries:
> Courage for the fearful,
> strength for the weak,
> the blind, the deaf, the mute
> will see and hear and speak!

Ten days till Christmas and the prophet cries:
> Return, rescued people,
> come to God in song,
> in everlasting joy,
> stay where you belong.

Ten days till Christmas and here are our cries:

> *(The congregation call out their own cries.)*

THE OTHER CHRISTMAS TREES (YOUNGER RETELLING)

Only ten days to go till Christmas! Here's a question we might not be thinking about: what plants or flowers do you know that have something to do with Christmas?

(Hear any suggestions from the children – maybe holly and ivy, mistletoe, Christmas trees … someone might even say poinsettia!)

We're going to hear about two other trees that are special at Christmas. They both grow in places that you wouldn't think trees can grow! One grows in the desert, and one grows on steep rocky mountain slopes. What amazing trees, one being able to grow where it's very hot and very dry, and the other one growing high up on slopes where the ground is hard.

Both of these trees produce a milky, gooey juice from the bark of their trunks. The one in the desert oozes its goo naturally. The one on the mountain has to have its trunk cut with a knife first. When the milky juice oozes out of the tree trunk and comes into contact with the air, it soon turns hard. Then the hardened lumps can be cut off the trunk and collected in a basket.

The lumps from the desert tree can be made into medicines to help ease all kinds of problems. It will help you if you get toothache, or a cold sore, or a sore throat, and it will reduce the pain of a bad bruise.

The lumps from the mountain tree have lots of good uses too. They can be made into medicine for coughs and colds. They contain an oil that will help anyone who is feeling very anxious, or they can be made into a skin lotion that can be used to treat spots. They also make a medicine that will ease your tummy if you have indigestion.

What amazing trees, making so many good and helpful medicines and oils – and they both grow in places where lots of other plants can't grow!

So what do they have to do with Christmas? Well, in the story of the first Christmas, it says that the medicine or oil from these two trees was given as the first Christmas presents! Can anyone guess what they are now? …

Frankincense and myrrh!

This Christmas, we probably won't get any frankincense or myrrh. We probably won't give someone a medicine for a cold or a lotion for a bruise! But what could we give that would make someone feel better in other ways? Any ideas? …

(Hear any suggestions from the children – smiles, hugs, compliments, a helping hand, playing together, saying thank you … and affirm that these might be the best Christmas presents to give and receive!)

Isaiah 40:1–11

HOW CAN I SAY IT?

A monologue of angst and prayer from Isaiah before he addresses the people. This should immediately precede the Bible reading, and flow into the reading. Both the monologue and prophetic message should be delivered passionately!

It's not easy being a prophet. It's not easy when God wants to speak and I'm the one who has to be God's voice. Uggh … how am I going to tell my family and friends and neighbours and nation that God is about to do something new? God is on the way to help us! Better times are ahead! But how can I persuade anyone to believe that? We've been stuck in this land so far away from home for such a long time. Lord, I know you want to encourage us! I know you're going to let us see you're with us – you're going to come in all your glory! But how can anyone trust that right now?

Look at this place. Nothing but wilderness. Steep rugged slopes … hot, dry valley beds … sand that makes us stumble and sheer rocks that make us slip. There's nothing here to speak of promise. Even the grass and shrubs sprout and wither from one day to the next. What do the shepherds find for their flocks? Who would lead the newborn lambs to this? No wonder we feel so doubly lost and cut off … exiled.

But not for much longer! Not for ever! All this is about to change. I know you're coming, God our mighty friend! How can I help them see it? How can I turn all their fears to hope, all their shame to dignity? Will you give me the words, Lord, to touch the wilderness inside … ?

Here they are, waiting for me. Right … deep breath …

GOD'S HELP IS COMING! (YOUNGER RETELLING)

A long, long time ago there lived a man called Isaiah. Isaiah was really good at cheering people up! All his friends and neighbours had been sent away from home to live in a country far away. They had plenty to feel sad about. Most of all they felt sad because they were worried that God had forgotten them. Maybe God was angry with them. Maybe God didn't care about them any more. But Isaiah knew that wasn't true! So he often prayed to God and said, 'God, how can I cheer up my friends again? What can I say to them? How can I help them to trust that you're going to come and help us?' And Isaiah always found a way to put a smile on people's faces again. 'Oh yeah,' they said, 'remember what Isaiah told us? God's not angry. God's not forgotten us. God's going to come and help us – soon!' So even though they were still in that faraway country, and they still didn't know quite what God was thinking of doing that would help them, somehow life didn't feel all that bad, not after they listened to Isaiah.

If you were Isaiah, what would you say to cheer the people up? I wonder if you've ever tried to cheer up a friend of your own who was sad. What was making them sad and how did you try to help? Or can you remember someone saying something nice to you when you were sad?

(Encourage the children to share some stories of their own.)

Isaiah 63:7–9 (Advent 1)

A YEAR OF THANKS

Prepare a selection of good news stories, each summarised in a brief paragraph, one from each month of the year – for ideas, see the Sunny Skyz and the Global Good News websites: www.sunnyskyz.com/good-news, www.globalgoodnews.com. Give one story each to 12 readers of any age, or two each to six readers, or three each to four readers, or share them out as possible! Intersperse these with brief retellings of events which the congregation, whether personally or communally, have been thankful for through the year. There are many ways you could make this storytime a symbolic recollection and thanksgiving for the year now ending. Here are a few possibilities:

> *The 12 readers stand around the walls or edges of the worship space, like a clock-face formation, with December being '12 o'clock' at the front/chancel. They read in turn and the congregation turn to face the reader, so they eventually turn a full 360 degrees, evoking the sense of the Earth faithfully revolving each day. Or people could process around the perimeter of the space, pausing to hear the stories (which would be read continuously), and in silence or aloud, name or share a story of their own.*

> *If fewer readers, have them stand at 3, 6, 9, 12 of clock-face formation.*

> *Sing a chant such as 'Ubi caritas' (Church Hymnary 4, 800), 'Alleluia' (CH4 751), 'Iona Gloria' (CH4 761) or another short song of thanksgiving. Sing after each three months/three stories have been read.*

> *Other options: Readers could each hold a large lit candle. They could have an old calendar page for their month, which could be held up with the good news story printed on the reverse side for them to read.*

JEREMIAH

Jeremiah 33:14–16 (Advent 1)

PROMISES, PROMISES

Prepare placards in advance, as simply or elaborately designed as you choose; use at least A2 paper. You will need 21 placards in all, in seven sets of three, with one of each statement below, with its two corresponding 'Oh yes ...' and 'Oh no ...' placards, ideally in a different colour.

1. (A) Things can only get better. (B) Oh yes, they can! (C) Oh no, they can't!

2. (A) There will be justice in this land. (B) Oh yes, there will! (C) Oh no, there won't!

3. (A) Our leader will run this country honestly. (B) Oh yes, s/he will! (C) Oh no, s/he won't!

4. (A) Everything will be all right. (B) Oh yes, it will! (C) Oh no, it won't!

5. (A) God is as good as his word. (B) Oh yes, God is! (C) Oh no, God isn't!

6. (A) We will all live in safety and security. (B) Oh yes, we will! (C) Oh no, we won't!

7. (A) There are lots of things you can be sure of. (B) Oh yes, there are! (C) Oh no, there aren't!

Use the placards immediately after the reading from Jeremiah, as follows:

Leader: These were fine words from the prophet all those years ago!
            But what if we heard those same sentiments
            proclaimed to us today?
            Just how would it all sound to us now, and would we agree?

1A: *(coming up front, or standing up wherever they are, holding placard high)*
            THINGS CAN ONLY GET BETTER!

1B: *(holding placard up)*
Say it with me, all you who agree!
OH YES, THEY CAN!

1C: *(holding placard up)*
Let's hear it if you're with *me*!
OH NO, THEY CAN'T!

2A: *(coming up front, or standing up wherever they are, holding placard high)*
THERE WILL BE JUSTICE IN THIS LAND!

2B: OH YES, THERE WILL!

2C: OH NO, THERE WON'T!

(... and so on, allowing everyone to voice their agreement or disagreement with each statement, panto-style. This could be done with 21 different placard-holders, or with three people doing them all in sequence. The concluding brief discussion question is optional, or you could pose a different question as you think appropriate.)

Leader: What, then, is promised for us now? What can we trust for today? I invite you to share your thoughts on that for a couple of minutes with your neighbours.

Jeremiah 36:1–28; 31:31–34

BURNING TRUTH

Jeremiah: Right, Baruch, let's go over what's happened. First, you went to the temple?

Baruch: Yes. I took the scroll and waited while the people gathered. Then I read it to them.

Jeremiah: All of it?

Baruch: All of it, yes. It took quite some time.

Jeremiah: And they listened? How did they seem to react?

Baruch: If anything, the crowd grew closer – and bigger –
the more I read.
It was a fast day, but the rumour is that
even those who have never fasted with much sincerity before,
have been fasting now for more than a day.

Jeremiah: A good sign then. A sign of change.

Baruch: Yes. A real desire for the Lord.
A recognition of the need to return to God's ways.

Jeremiah: Then the officials heard about it?

Baruch: That's right.
They could not have been unaware of the talk,
the very public shows of penance.
Some people were weeping in the temple all night!
One of the officials reported to a meeting of the court staff
at the palace.

Jeremiah: And they called you in?

Baruch: Yes. I was asked to read it all a second time, to the officials.

Jeremiah: But they reacted somewhat differently from the townspeople?

Baruch: Yes. They were alarmed; unnerved.
When I'd finished reading, they just stared at me,
and at each other, for a long time.
It was a very uncomfortable silence.

Jeremiah: Were you afraid, my son?

Baruch: It was what I expected.
These are harder words for our leaders to hear than the people.
It is harder for them to listen and to change.
Even when it is the Lord speaking, not you or I.

Jeremiah: What did they say? What broke their silence?

Baruch: Several of them began to mutter all at once, saying,
             'We must tell the king. The king must know of this!'

Jeremiah: But they didn't want you to be the one to read to the king?

Baruch: No. They took the scroll away from me.

Jeremiah: And let you go?

Baruch: They gave me a piece of advice first.

Jeremiah: Oh?

Baruch: That's when they said we should go into hiding.

Jeremiah: Ah yes. Well, no harm in heeding that, is there?

Baruch: I've had word that they are looking to arrest us.

Jeremiah: Yes, yes. But tell me again about what happened
             when they read to the king.
             What is it you heard?

Baruch: It was Jehudi who read the scroll to the king.
             He was in the winter palace.
             You know how cold these nights are, this time of year …

Jeremiah: Yes. So the fire was lit.

Baruch: That's right. The fire was lit.
             And every time the scroll was hanging down
             beyond Jehudi's elbow,
             the king lunged for it with a knife, ripped the end off
             and threw it in the fire.

Jeremiah: But what did all the others do? Do you know?
             Did they just stand by?

Baruch: No! They tried to stop him. They begged the king to stop!

Jeremiah: How brave.
             They must have known
             they were risking their lives …

That is a hopeful sign, a very hopeful sign.

Baruch: Yes, but they couldn't stop him. Not the king.
He paid no attention to their protests.
He ripped and burned the whole scroll. All of it!
All of the Lord's words to us!

Jeremiah: That means just one thing then.

Baruch: It means the Lord's message is gone.

Jeremiah: No. God will find deeper ways to get through to us, I'm sure.
We don't need written words to know what's right and wrong.
The king can burn scrolls and arrest prophets,
but he can't take away the call for change.

Baruch: But how will the people hear that call now?

Jeremiah: Until the Lord shows another way,
we'd better get back to writing.

Baruch: What? Do it all again?

Jeremiah: You wrote it all once,
and have read it out completely twice through, my son,
and I know the strength of your memory. And mine.

Baruch: You're right. We know much of it by heart.
All right. Take two, here we come.

JAMES DOESN'T LISTEN (YOUNGER RETELLING)

James loved chocolate. He especially loved the chocolate crispies Grandad made. Whenever Grandad visited, he brought a few chocolate crispies for James and Dad. Dad used to put them in a biscuit tin and put the tin in the kitchen cupboard under where the kettle sat. It was very easy for James to reach the chocolate crispies there. Dad had a special rule about not eating too much chocolate, but James didn't listen. Sometimes, when Dad was busy outside, James opened the cupboard, took the lid off the biscuit tin and took a chocolate crispie. He pulled down his jumper sleeve to hide it in his hand, and ran to his bedroom to eat it quickly before Dad found out. But Dad always seemed to know. He had told James time and again not to take a chocolate crispie unless Dad gave him one. Eventually Dad put the biscuit tin high up in a different cupboard, up above where the kettle sat. James couldn't reach it. Huh!

But one day James had an idea. He crept into the kitchen when Dad was in the garden. As quietly as he could, James pulled a chair over beside the cupboard, climbed up onto the chair, and stood up. Hurrah! He could reach the cupboard. He opened the door and looked for the biscuit tin. There was a pot of marmalade in front of it. James lifted the marmalade and put it down beside the kettle. Then he reached for the biscuit tin. He could just lift the lid and squeeze a hand inside without taking the whole tin out of the cupboard. He could feel the chocolate crispies under his fingers, so he grabbed one, pushed the lid back on, put the crispie in his sweatshirt pouch, put the marmalade back, closed the cupboard, climbed off the chair, pushed it back to the table, and ran off happily to his bedroom.

Dad didn't find out! Well, he certainly didn't say anything. So James did the same thing the following weekend, and the one after that. Still, Dad said nothing. He couldn't have known! James felt really pleased with himself. Although he'd given himself a fright the third time he took a crispie. The chair had wobbled and he had nearly dropped the marmalade pot! Luckily he didn't fall.

The week after that, he was playing football with Dad in the garden.

'James, is that chocolate on your face?'

'No, Dad.'

'Are you sure? James, do you understand why I want you to only have chocolate when I say so?'

'Yes, Dad, because it's not good to have too much chocolate. It's bad for my teeth and my tummy to have too many sweet things.'

'That's right. And if you tried to get the crispies from that high cupboard, you could have a fall and hurt yourself.'

'I know, Dad.'

But James wasn't really listening. Grandad's chocolate crispies were so delicious! Why should James always have to wait until Dad gave him one? The next weekend, he crept into the kitchen as usual, pulled over the chair, climbed up, opened the cupboard, and picked up the marmalade. Ooops! The chair didn't feel too steady and James had both hands on the marmalade pot. He felt himself leaning to one side as he lost his balance. He let go of the pot and tried to grab the cupboard door to stop himself falling but it was too late. The marmalade pot crashed to the floor, the chair wobbled over, and James landed on his side on the kitchen floor with a thump. He let out a yell and burst into tears. In no time at all, Dad was there, scooping him up and hugging him tight. 'James, are you all right? Where does it hurt?'

'I'm sorry, Dad! I'm sorry. My leg's sore!'

James had a big bruise coming up, and lots of sticky marmalade on his jeans and shoes. How he wished he had listened to Dad and done what he was told.

You could ask the children if they have ever behaved like James, and then wished they had listened.

Ezekiel

Ezekiel 37:1–14

BONES

Percussion instruments are given out before the story and a reader other than Ezekiel/God introduces the story, saying something like: 'Our story today tells of a vision God gave the prophet Ezekiel, at a time when God's people were feeling pretty hopeless because they were in exile, far from their homeland. Get ready to join in as Ezekiel leads us – because we are all going to be part of enacting the vision today! It all begins in a strange and deserted place …'

Ezekiel: *(quite pensive at first, rhythmic from start, but pace can be slow)*

> What **is** this **place**
> where **I'm** being **led**?
> What **is** this **place**,
> this **va**lley of the **dead**?
> No **sign** of **life**,
> no **ri**ver**bed**.
> What **is** this **place**,
> this **va**lley of the **dead**?
> So **emp**ty **there's**
> no **sense** of **dread**.
> What **is** this **place**,
> this **va**lley of the **dead**?
> No **vul**ture **flies**,
> no **in**sect **groans**,
> **no**thing **here**
> but **all** these **BONES**!

> *(Pause, look around slowly, keep whispering 'bones' while 'surveying' all the bones on the ground, in every direction. Resume rhythm slightly faster …)*

> These **bones** so **old**,
> these **bones** so **dry**,
> a**cross** the **va**lley
> **floor** they **lie**.
> A**head**, be**hind**,

bones **fill** the **eye**,
these **bones** so **old**,
these **bones** so **dry**.

God: *(quite dramatically, as if interrupting Ezekiel)*

These **bones** so **old**,
so **dead**, so **dry**,
these **bones** can **LIVE** –
now **pro**phe**sy**!
Breath, **flesh** and **skin**
I **will** sup**ply**.
These **bones** WILL **LIVE**!
Now **pro**phe**sy**!

Ezekiel: **Lis**ten, **bones**!
This **is** the **word**
of **God** who **is**
our **sov**ereign **Lord**!
Breath, **flesh** and **skin**
God **will** sup**ply**.
Bones, get **up**
and **come** al**ive**!

(Ezekiel begins to beat established rhythm on wooden blocks/
tambourine or suchlike, repeating phrase below and moving round
to bring in sections of congregation to add to rhythm on other
percussive instruments, by foot-tapping, handclapping, etc. May
need to give hand signal to lower volume before God continues
speaking, but keep rhythm going steady!)

Bones, get **up**
and **come** al**ive**!

God: These **bones** are **now**
raised **up** from **death**
with **flesh** and **skin**
but **still** no **breath.**
Com**mand** the **winds**
to **come** and **blow**.

Give **breath**, give **life**.
Let **it** be **so**!

Ezekiel: Come **winds**, come **breath**,
with**in** us **blow**!
God's **peo**ple, **rise**
and **have** new **hope**!

*(Ezekiel moves around sections of congregation again, repeating
phrase below and inviting folk to stand, move, jiggle, squirm,
process out of seats if so wished, etc. while keeping rhythm going.
May need to give signal to return to seats or stop where they are
before God continues speaking, but again, maintain rhythm.)*

God's **peo**ple, **rise**
and **have** new **hope**!

God: When **life** feels **dry**,
when **strength** turns **weak**,
when **hope** seems **gone**,
the **fu**ture **bleak**,
I'll **bring** you **back**
to **your** true **home**,
a **place** that's **good**
and **is** your **own**.
You will **know**
my **love** and **care**:
my **breath** with**in**
will **show** I'm **there**.

Ezekiel: Your **breath** with**in**
will **show** you're **there** …

*(Continued repetition of last line by all, Ezekiel gradually leading a
slowing down of pace, quietening of voices and tailing off of rhythm
into silence.)*

JOEL

Joel 2:23–32

THE AFTERMATH

Said as if surveying the devastated land after the locust swarm, with a mood of stunned shock and mourning. Should be read immediately before the Bible passage.

A: Is it over?

B: Have they gone?

C: Can I bear to look?

A: Oh ... my ... God.

B: Would you look at this.

C: I can't take in what I'm seeing.

A: The darkness – at least that's gone.

B: And the noise has stopped.

C: I've never known anything like it.

A: They were like fire crackling.

B: Blotting out the sun.

C: Filling the air like a crazed silver blizzard.

A: Covering the land, settling and soaring up
        on field and vineyard and orchard,
        whirling like dead leaves in an autumn storm.

B: Buzzing wings and cutting teeth, millions of them,
        scorching the earth with no mercy.

C: Their power and ferocity overwhelmed us,
        and we stand mocked by creatures we could crush by the fistful
        and trample underfoot.

A: There was corn ripe for harvest here, tall and gold.

B: There were grapes weighing down the branches of the vine.

C: Over there, figs were swelling on the trees
      and clustered olives turning from green to black.

A: Our livestock were at pasture.

B: We had milk and meat enough to feast.

C: It was going to be a great day in the Temple.

A: We were holding up despite the poor rains,
      but these swarming armies came without warning
      and tore apart everything we planted and tended.

B: The fields – look at them – nothing but bare earth.
      Not one stalk of wheat left standing,
      not one ear of barley to be found in the dust.

C: The vines are stripped naked. The trees stand white and exposed
      without bark or foliage.

A: They came with the wind and descended like a plague.

B: They rushed against us, robbing and ravaging everything we had.

C: And we could do nothing … nothing … to stop them.

A: There will be no wine and no bread.

B: Do you hear the cattle bellowing with hunger?
      Like voices for our grief.

C: The priests hold night-long vigils but can only weep.

A: What can we do?

B: Bow our heads and spread out to God our useless empty hands,
      with nothing to offer but our broken hearts.

C: God, is there hope? Is there hope, even now?

JOEL AND HIS FRIENDS (YOUNGER RETELLING)

Joel the prophet lived a long time ago. He had the very important job of listening to God and telling his friends what God was saying, and of listening to his friends and telling God what his friends were saying.

Many of Joel's friends were farmers. There was Enan who grew corn. There was Abi who had a grapevine. There was Merari who took care of the olive trees. There were Asha and Zeb who planted tomatoes and cucumbers and melons and pomegranates. There was Ira the shepherd and Obed who kept cows. They worked hard growing food in their fields and looking after their animals. Every year they looked forward to harvest time. It was always so wonderful to cut the corn, milk the cows and pick all the grapes – and make wine and bread for a big feast to say thank you to God!

But one year, as harvest time was coming, there was a terrible disaster. A huge swarm of flying, buzzing insects came swooping over all the fields. Locusts! There were thousands of them! No – millions of them! They were everywhere! Joel could hardly go outside without locusts getting in his hair and under his feet, flying and buzzing all round. They were small creatures, but with their tiny sharp teeth they began to eat everything they could find. They munched Enan's corn and nibbled Abi's grapes. They chewed up Merari's olives and even gnawed the bark off the trees. They gobbled up Zeb and Asha's juicy fruits and tasty vegetables. Then they landed on the grass that the sheep and cows liked to eat, and they chomped all the grass too.

'Dear God!' cried Joel, 'we're going to starve! Look – the locusts have polished off all our food! They've scoffed the lot! They've wolfed down everything – there's nothing left for us to eat! Even the cows are mooing in hunger, and the sheep are bleating because their bellies are empty!'

'My dear Joel,' said God, 'tell everyone not to panic. I know this is a hard time for you. I am going to send plenty of rain to get the grass growing again. It won't be long before your fields are full of corn, and you're busy making wine and olive oil again. Everything that the locusts took away, I will give back to you in a new harvest. And I'll give you something more special than food – I'll give you my Spirit, so that you can dream of how wonderful the world can be!'

So Joel told his friends what God was saying. And instead of feeling scared and worried, Joel's friends trusted God's promise and looked forward to their new harvest and their wonderful dreams.

JONAH

Jonah 1 & 2

Sailors' tale

Ash: Hey, Mushi! Good trip?

Mushi: No. Not a good trip.

Ash: Oh? Rough waters?

Mushi: You could say that.

Ash: The news that came back yesterday
          was of an unusual calm after quite a storm.
          You got caught in it too then?

Mushi: Yes … yes, we did.

Ash: Well, it's not the first squally night and it won't be the last, eh!
          You've survived it again!

Mushi: This time was different, Ash.
          I don't want to sail those waters again as long as I live.

Ash: What do you mean?
          When has a storm ever rocked you?
          You handle the big boats better than anyone, in any weather!
          Of course you'll be back out there!

Mushi: No, I mean it, Ash.
          My sailing days are done.
          In fact, my living days are done.
          I'm done.

Ash: What's got into you, man?
          What happened out there?

Mushi: I've killed a man.

Ash: What?!

Mushi: You heard me. I'm a murderer.
          My days are up.

I'll pay for it, I'm sure.

Ash: What happened, Mushi?
         An accident, surely?

Mushi: I didn't mean it – I didn't want to do it,
         but he said it was the only way.

Ash: Mushi, stop!
         Stop and tell me what this is all about.

Mushi: Were you here the day we were loading up?
         Do you remember the wee guy running about the place?
         Nobody knew him.
         He heard we were heading west
         and he was desperate to come with us?
         So we let him on the boat at the last minute:
         he had good money for the ride.

Ash: The wee guy with the black goatskin and tassels on his coat?
         He can't have gone with you!

Mushi: Yep, that was him. And he was with us, yes.

Ash: Mushi, that's impossible!
         He showed up again yesterday.
         Well, we found him at dawn, asleep on the beach.

Mushi: That's impossible! Ash, I killed him!
         I threw him overboard!
         But he made me do it. The gods were angry with someone.
         The sea was going crazy.
         We tried to lighten our load by throwing over half the cargo,
         but it didn't help.
         Then he said it was his fault, and we all yelled,
         'What have you done, man?!'
         He just yelled that he was running away
         and that we had to throw him over
         or the storm would kill us all.
         We wouldn't do it. We tried to row back, we tried everything,
         but in the end it was me who did it.

I pushed him over the side, into the sea.
He disappeared, Ash, he went right under, gone, just like that.
I killed him. I killed that poor man.

Ash: This isn't making any sense …
Do you remember anything else about what he looked like,
what he was wearing?

Mushi: Yes. His headband. It was silk.
I was staring at it as he was shouting at me …

Ash: Silk? Purple silk? And his hair is still pure black but …

Mushi: … but his beard is going grey.

(Pause. They stare at each other in disbelief.)

Mushi: No! How could he have survived?
How did he get back here?

Ash: How much longer did the storm last?

Mushi: No time at all. He went under and the waters went still.

Ash: Wow! Who is his god?

Mushi: He called his god the Maker of heaven and earth.
Maybe he was right.
We made our offerings and promised our devotion.
Taking no chances, not after that.

Ash: He must have been saved, somehow.
There was nearly a beached whale to deal with too yesterday.
She must have been thanking the gods we were on hand!

Mushi: But the man? Where is he? I have to see him to believe this!

Ash: He wasn't for hanging around.

Mushi: Where did he go?

Ash: Nineveh, apparently.

Mushi: NINEVEH?! Out of the frying pan, into the fire!

Ash: That's exactly what I thought.
        Bit of a turnaround after heading west with you.

Mushi: Yeah. Bit of a turnaround …

SAILOR FRIENDS (YOUNGER RETELLING)

Some sailor friends went out to sea
and Jonah went along for the ride.
Some sailor friends went out to sea
and Jonah was trying to hide!

Oh no, hiding from God,
what a thing to do.
Oh no, hiding from God,
Jonah, how silly are you!

The sailor friends got caught in a storm –
whoosh! how the rain and wind blew!
The sailor friends got caught in a storm.
'Oh, Jonah, is God mad at you?'

'Oh yes, God's mad at me!
I didn't do what he said!
Oh yes, God's mad at me,
I ran away instead!'

The sailor friends picked Jonah up
and threw him out with a 'plop!'
The sailor friends picked Jonah up
hoping the storm would stop.

'Oh no, what have we done?
Into the sea he goes.
Oh no, what have we done?
Will he survive? Who knows?'

The sailor friends came home from sea
and couldn't believe their eyes.
The sailor friends came home from sea
and Jonah was there – alive!

Oh yes, saved by a whale,
not drowned in the deep and dead.
Oh yes, saved by a whale,
to go and do what God said!

Micah

Micah 5:2–4 and 6:6–8

HOW SHALL WE COME?

Originally written for Remembrance

A reflective and provocative angle on where we might stand now in relation to Micah's words. The five voices symbolise our response in community.

1:    With what shall we come before the Lord?

2:    We come with grief at the fighting that sees no end.
      We come with despair at the wars upon wars.
      We come with longing for all conflict to cease ...

1:    With what shall we bow before God on high?

3:    We bow with sorrow.
      We bow with guilt.
      We bow with the knowledge of our warring ways.
      We are bowed by the violent, unkind, divisive words we have spoken;
      the arguments we have fuelled;
      the sparks of malice we have not extinguished;
      the injustices we have silently witnessed and walked on by ...

1:    Shall we come before God with burnt offerings?

4:    Burnt cities, burnt homes, burnt military targets, burnt schools ...

1:    Will the Lord be pleased with thousands of rams?

3:    Thousands of missiles, thousands of guns,
      thousands upon thousands upon thousands of dollars ...

1:    With ten thousand rivers of oil?

5:    Rivers of oil, rivers of blood, rivers of tears ...

1:    Shall we give our firstborn for our transgressions?

2:    And our secondborn and our thirdborn,
      the little ones and the forgotten ones,

the unnamed ones and the unmourned ones,
and how many more will die for our transgressions? …

1:    Shall we give the fruits of our bodies for the sins of our souls?

4:    Our children's lives for our inability to dwell in peace …?

1:    God has told us, mortal as we are, what is good.

5:    What is wholesome, what is fine,
what is constructive, what is life-giving,
what is hopeful, what is beautiful …

1:    What does the Lord require of us?

4:    Need from us, plead with us, demand of us, insist upon, implore us …?

1:    To do justice,

3:    rebalance the inequalities, redistribute the resources,
recalibrate the power,
until the cry is 'Life IS fair!'

1:    Love kindness,

2:    cherish the voices that speak gently,
honour the hands that help,
emulate the hearts that are open,
follow the feet that walk the extra mile,
celebrate the time that is shared generously.

1:    Walk in humility,

3:    knowing we don't know it all,

5:    there is always more to learn,

2:    we need each other,

4:    we are made for community,

2:    great leaders are great servants,

5:      and peace is not,

2, 3:   peace is not,

All: peace is not an impossible dream.

THREE THINGS TO DO (YOUNGER RETELLING)

A long time ago, there was a prophet called Micah who said there are three things people do that make God very very happy. He said God is very very happy when we are fair to each other, and when we are kind to each other, and when we treat everyone as equally important. But Micah could see that people aren't always fair and kind and good at treating others as equally important. I wonder when you have seen something happen that made you say, 'That's not fair!' Or something that made you say, 'That's not nice!' Or have you ever seen someone behaving as if they're better than everyone else, and you wanted to say, 'I'm just as important as you!'? *(Invite the children to share examples of their own for each situation. If possible, act them out.)* What if we could change the situation so that everyone could say, 'Yes, that's fair!' and 'Yes, that's nice!' and 'Yes, we're all important!' *(Talk through and act out the changed scenarios, where people behave fairly, kindly and show that all are equally important.)*

HABAKKUK

Habakkuk 1:1–4; 2:1–4

CLIMBING

Could either be read before the Bible passage, or as an interruption to the Bible passage, between Hab 2:1 and 2:2.

If all else fails, climb. Everything changes when I climb. I don't know why it makes a difference, but it does. I never know what I expect to see, but nothing looks the same from somewhere higher. A hillside. A rooftop. A tree. A tower.

It is a hard place down there on the level. The level? That's the last word for it. Who would choose to live in these times? How did we allow this? Did we bring it on ourselves? Did we get complacent, faithless, proud?

When my neighbour goes to court, can he not expect a fair hearing any more? Is every judge corrupt? Has wealth become prized over compassion? Is violence now the answer to every disagreement? We are turning into our own oppressors, never mind the powers that threaten from Babylon.

Who will be next to disappear from the streets? Whose child will be the next orphan? Which of us will survive, or will we be picked off one by one, two by two, enslaved and humiliated?

Yet God says nothing. God does nothing. Nothing changes. But when I climb, everything changes. I have to come here. I have to just keep getting up to a higher place. How small the city is and how broad the land from here. The fir tree and the stork live in harmony. The lion in all its wild energy does not turn on its own kind. The smell in the air is of flowers not fear. Here, heaven remains silent but the earth speaks. And the earth is still the Lord's.

Morning follows night and again I climb and I stay a while and I wait and God takes no heed of my cries. How much longer?

HABAKKUK THE PROPHET (YOUNGER RETELLING)

*You could devise and teach simple actions for the repeated 'Climb, climb, climb'
bit of the story.*

Habakkuk the prophet of God
was feeling frustrated and sad,
because everywhere he looked,
he saw people being bad!

'Dear God, there's someone fighting!
And there's someone telling lies!
Why is no one being kind?
Where are all the good guys?

'And where can I go to listen
to see what God will say?
I'm going to climb the tower,
to watch and wait and pray.'

*So let's climb, climb, climb the tower
to watch and wait and pray.
Up, up, up to the top
to see what God will say.*

Habakkuk listened hard.
Habakkuk listened well.
He pleaded for God to answer.
'God, say something!' Habakkuk yelled.

For a long time, God was quiet.
But Habakkuk climbed every day
up to the top of the tower
to see what God would say.

*So let's climb, climb, climb the tower
to watch and wait and pray.
Up, up, up to the top
to see what God will say.*

At last God gave an answer!
'Habakkuk, write this down,
keep it plain and simple
for everyone in town!

'Good things are going to happen!
Badness won't win the day.
Keep trusting me, I'm with you,
everything will be OK!'

Malachi

Malachi 3:1–4 (Advent 2)

SOAP OPERA

Invite seven volunteers to read out the following taglines from washing powder advertising. (Correct at time of writing; do check for any changes!) If possible, bring samples of each brand. See if people in the congregation can name the brand from the tagline. Have a vote on which tagline sounds the most convincing for good washing results. You could then have a brief washing contest, scrubbing similarly mucky pieces of white cloth or suchlike in soapy basins/buckets of each brand. Is there a clear winner?!

Then give people a few minutes to chat in threes and fours to come up with a product name and tagline for how God acts as an effective 'cleaning agent' personally and communally. Have fun with this! For example: 'Soapy Spirit: deals with the daily grime every time'. Invite people to share their ideas. Choose winners and give prizes if you wish – prizes must be soap of course! To finish, simply pose the question of what we wish would be 'washed out' of us as we approach Christmas, so that we can focus on what's precious. Encourage people to ponder that question and pray with it in the week ahead.

'Brilliant cleaning and long-lasting freshness' (ARIEL)

'Enjoy huggable freshness' (BOLD)

'Cleans deep down dirty; cleans your clothes and pleases your nose' (DAZ)

'Huggably soft for sensitive skin' (FAIRY)

'Mighty on cleaning; irresistibly soft and fragrant clothes' (PERSIL)

'Just-washed freshness that lasts and lasts' (SURF)

'For a brilliant clean every time' (TIDE)

ZEPHANIAH

Zephaniah 3:14–20 (Advent 3)

LOVE SONGS

As people come into church, give everyone a short piece of thin ribbon, an A5 piece of coloured paper (ideally with love hearts and musical notes in one corner or as a border, either pre-printed or using sticky shapes) and a pen or pencil if they don't have one.

Before the reading from Zephaniah, invite people to think of lyrics from love songs old and new, where the wonder of the beloved and the delight taken in them is being expressed in the first person. Give a few examples if you wish. Ask people to write a few of these endearing lines on their piece of paper, roll it up and tie it with the ribbon. Gather these in baskets.

After the Bible reading (not necessarily immediately) draw attention to Zephaniah's amazing words about God singing songs of love over us! Send round the baskets again and invite everyone to take a scroll and read the words they receive as God's expression of love for them.

LOVING WORDS (YOUNGER RETELLING)

Invite the children to share stories and ideas about expressing love. Write down some of their responses and repeat them back, making a big list of loving phrases.

Can you remember a time when somebody told you they love you? Maybe they didn't actually say 'I love you' but that's what they meant. What other words mean 'I love you'? What's the nicest thing a best friend has ever said to you? What's the kindest thing you've heard someone say about you? What things do your parents or grandparents or teachers say that make you feel really happy and special? What would you say to a friend if you wanted to make them smile and feel good? Do you know any songs people sing to say that they love someone?

Long ago a man called Zephaniah discovered that God sings songs to say how much he loves us! I wonder if God sings to us just the kind of nice loving things we say or sing to each other. Let's use some of the words we've thought of and sing them to each other just like God singing to us!

Susanna

Susanna 1–64

THE TWO JUDGES

How do you deal with behaviour like this?
Two men – elders and judges.
Seeing a woman, yet not seeing Susanna at all.
Watching her. Stalking her. Wanting her.
Ignoring their consciences.
Feeding their fantasies.
Shameful and secretive,
but eager to overpower her,
hungry to have her.
Hatching a plan, hiding and waiting,
cunning predators,
demanding compliance,
threatening violation,
blackmailing in the face of refusal –
if she won't give in, she'll have no way out.

Trapping her knowingly,
lying intentionally,
manipulating with no regard for her life.
Innocence shredded –
husband, parents, children, servants, all taken in.
Abusers believed.
How do you deal with behaviour like this?
Preying on, trapping, discrediting, condemning.
How do you deal with behaviour like this?

Caught out at the last –
stopped, examined, exposed, convicted.
Justice done.

It doesn't often end so well.

THE TWO JUDGES (YOUNGER RETELLING)

This is a story from a long time ago, about two men who were supposed to be kind and honest people. They had an important job to do, being judges. That meant knowing what is right and wrong and helping everyone else to behave kindly and honestly. But the two judges did not behave well themselves. They began to bully a woman called Susanna.

One day they hid in Susanna's garden and waited until she was all alone. Then they tried to make her do things she didn't want to do. They wanted to touch her and kiss her and take her clothes off. Susanna got very upset because they wouldn't leave her alone. 'Do what we want!' they cried. When Susanna said no, they decided to tell lies about her. They told Susanna's family that they had seen her in the garden, kissing and cuddling a strange man who was not her husband. Susanna's husband and her children and her parents and her servants all believed the men's lies. They believed Susanna had done the things the judges said, but she hadn't! She had done nothing wrong!

The two judges didn't even care when they saw that Susanna was about to be punished. But suddenly, one boy in the crowd called Daniel stood up and said, 'Wait! Do we really know the truth yet?' Daniel had the feeling that maybe the two judges should be asked a few more questions.

So Daniel took the first judge away from the second judge and asked him, 'When you saw Susanna and the strange man in the garden, what kind of tree were they next to?'

'Let me think … it was a mastic tree,' said the first judge.

Then Daniel took the second judge away from the first judge and asked him, 'When you saw Susanna and the strange man in the garden, what kind of tree were they next to?'

'Let me think … it was an oak tree,' said the second judge.

Ooooooh … what do you think happened next? *Let the children finish the story!*

SOURCES AND ACKNOWLEDGEMENTS

Some of the pieces in this book were previously published in:

Fig Trees and Furnaces: Biblical stories, scripts and reflections – Esther to Maccabees, Ruth Burgess (Ed.), Wild Goose Publications, 2018

Olives and Obligations: Biblical stories, scripts and reflections – Genesis to Nehemiah, Ruth Burgess (Ed.), Wild Goose Publications, 2018

Spill the Beans. Spill the Beans material © the contributors. Spill the Beans is 'a lectionary-based resource with a Scottish flavour for Sunday Schools, Junior Churches and worship leaders': http://spillbeans.org.uk

Summer: Liturgical resources for May, June and July, including Eastertide and Pentecost, Ruth Burgess (Ed.), Wild Goose Publications, 2020